ignis

'*Bails and Boardrooms* is a considered reflection of the phenomenon that is David Nash; a whirlwind of actions, reactions, emotions, empathy and ideas. It is an easy and enjoyable read containing sage advice at a pace which makes you understand why time spent with Nashy is never dull or unforgettable.'

Angus Fraser, former Middlesex player and England Test selector

'Nashy is a character, which comes out in the book; and he's a great bloke, which you learn while turning the pages. Cricket doesn't allow for many bad 'uns and Nashy represents all the good ones – sense of humour, self-deprecation and honesty to the fore. That he has made such a successful 'second' life for himself is a tremendous achievement … and now the whole story, told from his heart. Is there no end to the man's ambition and achievement? Go Nashy …'

Mark Nicholas, broadcaster, writer and former cricketer

'An engaging story with real lessons from a life well-lived. Everyone can pick up a tip or two and reflect with the same honesty about what it takes to taste success, to get through the harder moments in life and ultimately be happy in your own skin. Both Bails and Boardrooms would benefit from a few more like Nashy!'

Penny Hughes, CBE, Business Leader

'A rare combination of humour, honesty and great nuggets of wisdom as Nashy uses these pages to take us on his personal journey through fame, fear and ultimately fortune.'

Michael Tobin, OBE,
Technology Entrepreneur and Philanthropist

'*Bails and Boardrooms* was a very easy and really enjoyable read. It provided a powerful mix of humour, wise words and tales from a top professional sportsman. Most importantly, it highlighted the need to talk and understand more about mental health and an awareness of how it can affect even an outward-going "Top Dog" like Nashy.'

Nigel Oddy, Business Leader

BAILS AND BOARDROOMS

DAVID NASH

BAILS AND BOARDROOMS

DAVID NASH

How Cricket Changed My Life

Foreword by Sir Andrew Strauss

pitch

First published by Pitch Publishing, 2021

Pitch Publishing
A2 Yeoman Gate
Yeoman Way
Worthing
Sussex
BN13 3QZ
www.pitchpublishing.co.uk
info@pitchpublishing.co.uk

A CIP catalogue record is available for this book from the British Library.

ISBN 978 1 78531 764 4

Typesetting and origination by Pitch Publishing

Printed and bound in India by Replika Press Pvt. Ltd.

Contents

To Mum, Dad, Glen, Jules and my girls.

xxx.

With thanks to cricketarchive.com
for the scorecards

Foreword

Sir Andrew Strauss OBE

WALKING INTO the Middlesex dressing room in the late 1990s was intimidating to say the least. The club itself, the club of Brearley and Compton, Haynes and Gatting, has a rich history full of trophies and legends. Being based at Lord's, the home of cricket and the citadel of the game adds to the feeling of grandeur associated with Middlesex. For a young aspiring cricketer like myself, I was both in awe and disbelief that some of my heroes growing up were suddenly on the same payroll as me. The feats of Mike Gatting, Angus Fraser, Phil Tufnell and Mark Ramprakash had all been indelibly marked on my mind as I watched England battle through my formative years with some stunning victories that seemed to put a smile on the face of the nation. Contrast that with some horrifying defeats that sent sports editors thumbing through their thesauruses to find new superlatives to describe England's latest humiliation.

In my early days at Middlesex I felt a little like Charlie Bucket when he got his ticket to visit the chocolate factory. It was glorious to be a contracted professional at Middlesex, but I felt somewhat out of place and undeserving. In truth my cricketing pedigree was pretty much non-existent. I was not one of these superstars from the junior ranks who had been earmarked for a long and successful England career, and my mediocre exploits for Oxfordshire Under-19s had done little to get the seasoned veterans at Lord's excited.

In complete contrast to myself, Middlesex had two potential superstars on their books at that time. Owais Shah, whose extraordinary talent and ability shone with every shot he played, looked every inch an international player in the making. Alongside him was a wicketkeeper-batsman who didn't have quite the eye-catching shots of Shah, but possessed an extraordinary confidence in his game, a streetwise attitude to cricket, and an ability to out-chirp all the seasoned Middlesex England stars. That player was David Nash. In so many ways, David was completely unforgettable.

Nashy was the complete antithesis of me. He was exuberant, extroverted, at ease with his surroundings and utterly sure that he was going to make it as a pro. He loved a night out with his mate Richard Johnson, and yet was still able to back it up the next day on the pitch. I, on the other hand, was still wondering quite frankly why Don Bennett, the Middlesex coach, had decided to take a punt on such an unproven opening batsman. While Nashy was out on the lash in Kingston, I tended to be in my room writing in my journal and trying to prepare as well as I could. I can't tell you how dispiriting it was to see him effortlessly craft another 50 the next day, while I naively fell victim to the new ball. I envied Nashy's attitude almost as much as I envied his gift of the gab.

Fortunately for me, Nashy turned out to be the 'go-to' player to make new players at the club feel welcome, whether they be newly contracted cricketers or triallists who often were invited to make up the numbers when some of the second-team players were called away to play in the first team. As such I gravitated towards him and didn't mind him taking the piss out of me for being a 'jazzer' and not having a clue what I was doing. I came to increasingly enjoy my cricket when Nashy was around in the second team, and felt slightly bereft when he was whisked away to play in the first team at the tender age of 19.

My chance in the first team ironically came at the expense of Nashy, who had found life a little harder at first-team level, and had failed, probably for the first time in his life, during the 1998 season. By 1999, however, we were both in the first team, and over the next ten years we spent far too much time in the slip cordon, dressing rooms, cars, bars and nightclubs together often with our wives, Jules and Ruth.

Over the years, I began to appreciate that despite Nashy's brash exterior, he was a guy who thought deeply about life, and genuinely cared about those around him. This was most evident with his mum and dad, who were always there to support him. Nashy was always on hand to chat to players going through tough times, and he had a knack of being able to get people to open up to him about what they were really feeling about any particular situation. I counted on his support and wise counsel many times as I started to make my way in the international game.

It also became increasingly apparent over the course of our time playing together that Nashy was not quite the ultra-confident, happy-go-lucky person that he first appeared to be. Despite giving the impression that nothing fazed him,

I increasingly sensed that he was battling internally with the pressures of performing while all the while having to pretend to the world that he was completely unaffected. At first this anxiety presented itself with some of his strange match-time mannerisms (he developed an unhealthy habit of having to walk around the stumps a number of times at the end of every over), and over time this became more extreme to the extent that it was clear he was struggling to get quality sleep and get himself in the right frame of mind to perform.

Given that he was so much the heartbeat of the team, I and others went out of our way to check that he was okay, but he never gave too much away. Perhaps in his mind he was coming to terms with the fact that it was time to move on from cricket and embark on the next phase of his life.

Despite being extremely proud of his lack of academic credentials (an N and a U at A-level was actually quite an impressive feat!), it was always clear to me that Nashy would fall on his feet post-cricket. He had too much about him and was frankly too likeable to fade away into obscurity, only to be remembered for his feats on the pitch. What has been surprising, though, is to see an emergence of both passion and work ethic once he started D&G group with his brother Glen. If he had one weakness as a player, it would have been that the hard graft of cricket preparation always came second to the lure of a night out or a curry with his mates. It is clear that he has found his calling in life. He is running a business based on people, raising money for fantastic causes, and developing some wonderful customers and friends in the process.

While he has not sold his company for hundreds of millions of pounds and cannot be regarded as a titan of business yet, he may well be the right leader at the right time – post the COVID crisis, the world is turning away from transactional relationships and moving towards ideas, businesses and people who are driven by a passion, a principle and are willing to see it through. This book is testament to that.

This book is testament to that and I have been fortunate enough to see that generosity of spirit first hand over the last two years as I have struggled to come to terms with the loss of my wife Ruth from a rare form of non-smoking lung cancer. David's support, both personally and with the Ruth Strauss Foundation, which I set up following Ruth's death, have been completely invaluable. I am incredibly grateful that David has suggested that some of the proceeds from this book go towards the Foundation and our desire to provide professional support for families when preparing for the death of a parent from Cancer. The success of the Foundation is completely reliant on people who passionately believe in the cause, and we have no greater a supporter than David.

Whatever happens to David and his business going forward, one thing is guaranteed. He will be an unforgettable presence to so many people and will remain an extremely close friend.

Introduction

WRITING A book is a scary prospect for anyone. Writing this book was terrifying.

Of course, it forced me to put my ideas on the page for others to judge which is scary. Still, it terrified me because I wasn't sure if I could do it or whether I had anything interesting to say. Over the years, I've come to rely on people who know what they're doing. On that basis, I've got some talented and vital people to thank for getting me over the boundary ropes with this book. Firstly, Ed Smith; a top bloke, great cricketer, a bloody useful selector and a brilliant writer himself. Throughout, he's been a constant source of wisdom. As I began to think about writing this book, Ed sent me some advice which was gold. It acted as my guide from day one. Here is the text he sent:

> You made cricket work for you. Many players don't. Cricket defeats them because there is little for them afterwards. So whatever frustrations or poor behaviour you saw, you won at cricket in a way that few do. Because you went far beyond the game afterwards, it is beneath you to 'level' any lousy behaviour from ages ago. Churchill said that he wanted to 'take more out of alcohol than alcohol took out of him'. And I think that is one way to think about cricket. It should inform, inspire, clarify the life lived during and after playing the game. It's the life that matters. And we should – if we can – feel grateful that cricket gave us a rich and demanding set of circumstances during which we learned about life. Then those experiences must be put to good use – whether it is supporting charities, or starting a business, or selecting teams. The only way to win – long term – is to turn experiences into things of lasting value.

Here was a lesson for how I should approach this book but a lesson for life too. I measure my own life by the experiences I have, the friendships I make and the memories I cherish. Ed's note was a very good reminder of many of those things.

I must thank my cricket mates too. They tolerated endless questions about dates and details of the stories in this book. The presence of alcohol in some of those stories prevented me from remembering every detail. Finally, perhaps the biggest thank you of all goes to my great pal Garry Lace, or Lacey as I know him. He knows cricket, he knows a thing or two about business but best of all he knows me. All three of those things proved invaluable as he helped me craft the pages of this book. Without his skill, insight, sense of fun and ability to badger the f*** out of me, none of this would have happened.

They say that if you want to go fast, go alone but if you want to go far, go together. The pages that follow describe how far I've come personally and professionally. Whilst I wouldn't ever claim to have reached my destination yet, I couldn't have done any of it without everyone that has ever been with me on the journey. You all know who you are and I'm sorry that I can't name every single one of you. Thank you all from the bottom of my heart.

Writing this book is one of the most daunting things I've ever done. I've put myself, my business ventures, and what I think about what makes companies tick on the pages of a book that some people might read. If that's not evidence that life is a funny old thing, I don't know what is.

Chapter One

Opening Up

STANDING BEHIND the stumps that day, I knew I was in trouble. Not the usual type of scrape I'd find myself in after a night out with the lads. This was trouble of a very different kind. A kind of whirring in your brain that means it's hard to separate the senses. A sense that the world is about to implode around you. I forgot that I was in the middle of a game. Frightened, alone and unbelievably anxious, I heard the ball off the edge of the bat. The next thing I saw was the ball on the ground. I'd dropped Martin Love, Durham's Aussie overseas number 3, at a crucial stage of the game which was more crucially live on Sky. There was nowhere to hide.

Did I care that I'd dropped the catch? Not really. I cared about something much bigger in that moment. What everyone else thought about me. My parents, my mates, my brother, my missus, my kids and everyone involved in cricket, inside and outside of Middlesex. I was mentally shot to pieces and the game that I had loved for years had done that. So much so that, in the next over, I feigned injury so that I didn't have to put myself through the torture of another ball in front of the TV cameras.

The shame I felt walking off the pitch that day has never left me. It was also the day I finally had to admit that my cricketing days were numbered and that I was lying to myself and others. More importantly, it was the day that I was able to be honest with myself about the struggle that was to prove the biggest of my life – my mental health. Cricket had destroyed it and my journey since then is the story of battling those demons.

I was very average as a professional cricketer.

A funny thing to say given my 16-year career, but it's true. As luck (and hard work) would have it, I turned out to be a much better businessman. That's why I wanted to write this book. Why is it that sport and business have so much in common? What was it about my career in cricket that gave me the skill and the will to create my successful business ventures? These are some of the questions I've asked myself during the last decade. By the end of this book, I hope that you and I will have a few answers.

People and businesses make the world go round: sport, politics, our company (of which much more later). Almost everything else that I've come across in my 40-plus years on Earth revolves around these two things. Business people have always fascinated me. So have people who have achieved real success in businesses large and small. I like hearing the stories, making the contacts, and seeing the varied perspectives on life as an employer or employee. I love learning about new companies and new ways that people find to make pie and mash. That's cash to the non-private schoolers reading this. I enjoy discovering ways to develop new ideas, and I love seeing them come to fruition. I'm pretty good at seeing things through from start to finish. Even in my cricketing days, with the bat, I was good at seeing us over the line to win matches and I loved it best of all when I had to dig us out of the shit. It's no different now in my business life.

Over the years, advice from leaders I know has often steered me through choppy and dangerous waters, and these leaders have come from the worlds of both business and sport. The list of names of those I admire is too long for this part of the book, but their names will crop up on many of the pages that follow. Though I started my professional life batting, bowling and fielding, I was probably more born to business than I was to cricket. Still, our house backed on to Sunbury Cricket Club rather than the London Business School, so I guess the early writing was always on the wall for me. It was cricket first.

Lots of people told me that you have to start these kinds of books with a mix of funny stories from your childhood. Early pointers as to how things were always going to pan out and a forensic examination of events in your teenage years to explain why you turned out to be the person you are. If that's what you were hoping for in this chapter and indeed this book generally, I apologise now. Firstly, I'm not sure my life was ever that interesting when I was younger. Of course, Mum and Dad and my brother Glen were terrific. I had (and still have) a fantastic group of friends and family, but life-changing moments were few and far between when I was growing up in Sunbury. Secondly, I'm not a big fan of talking about myself, so I'm going to find it equally hard to write about myself. However, this book does mean that you'll have to suffer that occasionally.

Suffice to say – and only because I have to include some highlights – I was born on 19 January 1978 in Sunbury. It's a place I love and where I still live within a mile of Mum and Dad, my brother Glen and his family. My early years took in the sights and sounds of the local state schools. I went to Beauclerc, Chennestone, and then Sunbury Manor although in those days most people called it Scumbury Manor! Sport quickly became the centre of my and my brother's universe. In truth, Glen was a much better sportsman than me. Like me, he played cricket through the Sunbury and Middlesex age groups and with a bit more will on top of his skill, I may have been able to realise my dream of playing at Lord's with my brother. Despite his ability though, he just didn't want it enough as a youngster. At least that's what I thought until chatting to him as part of the research for this book. Glen admitted in that conversation that he never really wanted to follow in my footsteps or invite any comparisons with to me in that way.

My first significant memory of Middlesex was seeing them lose to Warwickshire in the dark in the 1989 NatWest Trophy Final. I was gutted but went on to the outfield for the presentation. I remember feeling the grass and thinking how amazing it was. I just couldn't stop touching it. I'd never have guessed that one day, I'd call that grass my home. By the age of ten, I was in the Millwall youth squad playing on the right of midfield and coached by the legend that was Les Briley. I always had great vision with the ball but no speed. Never helpful for the engine room of any team. Les himself played in midfield professionally, so I suspect he spotted quite quickly that my football career wasn't going anywhere.

I grew up developing a lifelong love of four sporting clubs; my beloved Sunbury CC would have to be top of that list of course. A club that was to be the catalyst for my career and some amazing lifelong friendships. When I wasn't at Sunbury, I used to go and watch Brentford with the First Sunbury Tuesday cub pack, with my best mates from school, Gareth Rees and Simon Pavitt. I still take my kids to Brentford now. Terry Evans was my Brentford footballing hero back then. He was so hard that even the scaffolding at the ground was scared of him. Kerry Dixon became my hero at Chelsea. What a striker that man was. My old man would take us to almost every home game, so it was hard not to fall in love with the Mighty Blues. Standing in the Shed End as a boy with Dad and his pals definitely taught me about the real world from a young age. It also gave me a good swearing vocabulary which I still like to use to this day. Last but by no means least in my list of clubs I love are the Middle Saxons as Mike Selvey (Middlesex president) would say. Middlesex County Cricket Club, a club that was to be such a massive part of my life, started with days off school sanctioned by the old man whenever there was a big game. Watching my heroes clutching one of my Mum's fabulous packed lunches and my autograph book are memories I'll never forget. Perhaps my dreadful GCSE results and lack of academic progress were something to do with the fact that I was never at school unless Middlesex were on a poor run.

My cricketing career started young. Guided by my Dad's passion for the game and the proximity of Sunbury CC to our house, I was in the nets most days after school. By the age of nine, my shaggy perm meant that I looked like a young Ryan Sidebottom. This didn't put off the legendary Frank Sharman from recommending me for Middlesex trials and I soon found myself in their junior set up. I once took six wickets in six balls for Sunbury Under-11s, the final wicket of which was a majestic caught and bowled. Well, at least that's how the old man described it from his position as umpire. It's tough to get six in six with your dad in the chair. I remember the first ball was plumb lbw, and he didn't want to give it, but he had no choice. It was going on to hit all three stumps. From then on, I made it easy for him. I rattled the stumps with the next four deliveries and then came that last magnificent catch I've just mentioned. Looking back now, it was probably my most significant achievement as a cricketer! Well, that and my hundred for Middlesex against the great spinner Murali's box of tricks some years later. My great mate, John Maunders, and I still talk about that game today given he got a ton for Leicestershire against Murali just a few weeks later.

When we get together, our party story is our batting exploits against one of the world's great spinners. We always manage to clear the room more quickly than usual with that one! The six from six though is certainly up there for me. Not least because a great chap called Hugh Goldie, chairman of Richmond CC and our opponents that day, arranged to have the ball mounted and inscribed for me some weeks later. It's those gestures that you never forget. One of my lasting memories of that day was that my Mum and Dad were over the moon. They loved their sport and still do. I owe them an enormous amount. In fact, I owe them everything, as does Glen. It's not possible in words to explain how much Mum, Dad and Glen have done for me. Blood is thicker than water, and I know there's nothing we wouldn't do for each other.

It's been one of the great privileges of my life to build a business with my brother. One of the reasons we've done well is that we've never had to worry about trusting each other to do the right thing. We've just had to worry about building a business and not losing our hair along the way. I guess that last bit didn't go so well. In all of our time working together, we've only had one major blow-up, and it's something I regret to this day. Not because of the disagreement we had but because of what I said to Glen at the time. I told him that he was nothing without me. Words in anger that weren't true then, and they are not true now. Glen is a great foil for me, in life and business. As Mum and Dad know already, I will never forget the things that they've done for us and the sacrifices they've made. We're a big family, they are both at the head of it, and we're so lucky to have them there. I hope they are proud of the people that Glen and I have become.

Although I hated school, my party trick growing up was anything to do with numbers. I was a teenage Carol Vorderman. Years later, this ability with numbers didn't help me when I was batting with Owais Shah. I think he must have missed a few maths lessons at school because he could never quite work out that an over was six deliveries. It's not easy to farm the strike with someone who can't count. Needless to say, we suffered the odd run-out or two when batting together, which never went down well.

I was picked for England aged 15 to tour South Africa. That squad contained the likes of Freddie Flintoff, Gareth Batty, Alex Tudor and David Sales. In my opinion, Salesy was the best batsman never to have played for England. Sadly, he never looked the part in a skin-tight shirt but he'd have been the first name on my England team sheet in that era. He was box office.

I loved everything about that first England tour. Freddie and I put on a partnership of well over 100 to win the Test at Newlands. Apart from Lord's, Newlands is still my favourite ground in the world. That tour also allowed me to experience a medical first. My room-mate, Gareth Batty, who was way more experienced and streetwise than me, woke up in the middle of the night in agony. It turned out that he had a twisted testicle and was in more pain than I've ever seen anyone in my life. Needless to say, the next day, the lads couldn't help wondering what we'd been up to. We certainly hadn't persuaded anyone to join us in our room despite our best efforts so goodness only knows what Bats was doing with himself that night. The mind boggles.

That tour finished on a real high for me – South Africa needing one to win in a day/night one-day game at Centurion Park in Pretoria. The batsman missed and I managed to throw down the stumps with both keeping gloves on to win the game and the series. I still have the orange stump to this day. Great memories were made and lifelong friendships formed. I was living the dream.

Having said that, things weren't always plain sailing. During the early years at Middlesex, I nearly got sacked by the county for streaking at Lord's while executing an almost perfect Jürgen Klinsmann dive on the sodden outfield. The £250 on offer to do it was never forthcoming, which taught me one of my most valuable life lessons: always try to get the money up front! I knew I was in real trouble that day when Tuffers (Phil Tufnell) put his arm around me after it happened and said, 'Don't worry, if they sack you dog, I'll back you.' Luckily, they backed me.

Years later, I was fortunate enough to be able to repay Tuffers the favour and back him in the jungle. Tuffers sat myself and Middlesex bowler Tim Bloomfield (a good pal of Tuffers at the time) down in the changing room to ask our advice about the ITV programme, *I'm a Celebrity, Get Me Out Of Here*. He was worried about doing the show and looking stupid. 'What if I get slung out first? I'll be a laughing stock.' My reply was clear and succinct. 'Tuffers, we've been training at Merchant Taylor's School in the freezing cold for the last two days whilst you've been making your own cheese and ham sandwiches and moaning like a good 'un. Go and do it. You'll win it.' The rest is history. Great advice from the Nash Dog for a change! Tuffers is one of the funniest blokes I know and was a bloody good bowler in his day too. I miss those days with him.

I lost most of my hair at 18 down various plug holes at Malvern College. I joined that school aged 16 on a sports scholarship and was lucky enough to play with some great blokes who were also very talented cricketers. Dan Walker, Gavin Franklin, Mark Hardinges and Simon Morgan all went on to play the game at some level, and I'd like to think I played my part in helping them get there. They are all still great mates, and we are lucky enough to have won five Cricketer Cups together as Old Boys. Tragically, Dan Walker lost his son, Theo, to a heart defect some years ago. So, through the work we do at D&G now, it's been an honour and a real privilege to have been able to support the Theo Walker Fund in recent times.

I had Don Bennett, the remarkable Middlesex coach, to thank for my Malvern scholarship. What a legend that man was. I also had him to thank for my debut given he turned out to be my lift to that game. Saturday, 16 September

1995 saw me playing football for Malvern against the mighty Millfield School at their ground in Somerset. Don came to watch that game specifically so that he could then give me a lift to Taunton to the team hotel for the final game of the AXA Equity & Law league season against Somerset the following day. I bagged my first three dismissals that game including stumping Mushtaq Ahmed and a catch off big Gus Fraser. Sunday, 17 September 1995 is a date that will be indelibly etched into my memory forever. Walking down the steps to make my debut at a packed Taunton ground with my hero, Mike Gatting, as captain really was the stuff of boyhood dreams.

The more I washed my hair at Malvern, the more it just kept falling out. As a result, I've looked like a bloke in my forties for the last 20 years of my life, but this didn't prevent me from meeting my amazing wife, Jules, at McCluskey's nightclub in Kingston. I loved a good cheesy 80s night as much as the next man and my average in that club was much better than at Lord's at the time! Jules has been by my side through thick and thin since then, and without her, there's no doubt that I'd be half the person I am today. She is an amazing woman. Grounded, straightforward, down to earth and for some reason best known to herself, she seems to love having me around. She's smarter than me, more organised and is the one with the looks in our partnership. She has believed in me more than almost anyone, and that alone has kept me going over the years. I'm a lucky man.

By the age of 25, I had developed significant mental health issues as a result of playing cricket, which have been with me ever since. The game messed with my head daily and caused massive levels of anxiety for me.

It's hard to imagine this now, but I used to get so anxious that I feigned injury to come off the field many times. I was at my happiest when it was raining and I was in the sanctuary of the dressing room playing cards with the lads. Or better still, looking at the weather forecast and seeing 100 per cent chance of rain the following day. That always meant that we could press the 'G' button as we called it. In other words, gambling on the forecast being right, us all getting lashed with a late night and a curry knowing that we didn't need to play the next day. Manchester was always good 'G' button fodder because it never stops raining there. We spent more time in Rectory Nightclub in Wilmslow than we did at Old Trafford. I was always more nervous opening my hotel room curtains than I was batting against Shoaib Akhtar, Courtney Walsh or Allan Donald!

I have already mentioned that game against Durham in front of the TV cameras. I dropped a catch early and just couldn't face another over. So, I pulled up while running to the stumps for an incoming throw and pretended to be injured (hamstrings were always good because the physios can't really detect what's what) so that I could come off. I'm not proud of it, but it does demonstrate how big a part anxiety played in my career.

The anxiety meant that I was also living a lie that eventually found me out. My biggest fear was realised when Ed Joyce (Joycey), the then Middlesex vice-captain under Ed Smith, outed me. He had realised that my feigning injury was total bollocks and pulled me up on it face to face. Initially, I told him he had lost the plot but he knew I was lying. This definitely affected our relationship and I'll never forget the day when, having been passed fit by the physio after one of my feigned hamstring injuries, I was then dropped.

I turned up at Lord's having been picked to play and in one of my better mental states. Ed Smith, our captain, was already in the nets as was his usual routine. I said my usual hello to Joycey in the changing room only to be questioned by him as to why I was there, which I thought very strange. However, I continued my usual pre-match routine and found myself practising next to Ed Smith in the adjoining net. Ed caught my eye and said, 'Dog, has no one mentioned that you're not playing today and that we're going with Ben Scott?' They obviously hadn't and I was furious. Not because I wasn't playing because Ed may have had good reason at the time, but I was livid with Joycey who had made me walk over to the nets and embarrass myself despite knowing the situation.

Having screamed at Joycey and told him what a back-stabbing c**t I thought he was, I went immediately to the CEO's office at the time with my pads still on and demanded a meeting with the chairman, Ian Lovett. When he eventually emerged, I didn't hold back on how poorly I'd been treated and what a shambles the club was. The least I had expected was to be told by the coach, John Emburey (one of life's great blokes), why I wasn't playing despite averaging over 50. It was perhaps the angriest I'd ever felt as a cricketer and Joycey and I never really recovered from it. Ironically, Ben Scott made a hundred that game which was the beginning of the end for me.

My mental health issues have been the hardest legacy of my playing days to overcome. I had talent as a sportsman but never really made the most of it. I loved the lads, the banter, and the beers. I still do. But, as my career drew to an end, I grew to hate playing the game most of the time. The mental well-being impact of a career in cricket could be the subject of an entire book in itself. Suffice to say that it will be a recurring theme in this one.

So, that's what you're going to get of David Nash through the ages for now. Other than Jules and my mum, no one ever calls me David. I've always been Nashy, whether in the changing room or the boardroom. Knocker's my other nickname, but the background to that isn't for these pages. This book is a family one, after all. I'll come back to some of these stories and share some others. Still, the real point of this book is to write about what drives me now and what has most influenced me over the years in helping me build my business. You could call it Nashy's manifesto for business (and life) if you like, based on what I've learned on and off the pitch. It won't be up there with Sir Alan Sugar or Warren Buffett, but it's the best I've got.

Chapter Two

My Story

THE LAST time I put on my wicketkeeping gloves for Middlesex was not the last day of my cricket career. It turned out to be the first day of the rest of my life. Cricket had been my life for over 25 years, but it had become much more than that. It was a literal and metaphorical training ground which had given me great highs and incredible lows. The highs of winning and then sharing a beer with your mates are moments you never forget, but it was the lows that ended up defining much of my career. The lows of losing are painful, but it wasn't those that led me to terrible anxiety and depression. The pressure of having to perform, combined with the sense of utter loneliness when I under-performed, took its toll. Mum and Dad did their best to take the edge off my bad days in my early years of living at home. Most of the time, it had the opposite effect. I felt their disappointment much more than my own. The occasional smashed window in their house was a testament to how the game affected me. Even thinking about those moments now makes me shudder.

That sense of loneliness makes cricket unique. It's a team game that most of the time, you play as an individual. I see the impact these issues have today on the many young players coming through, and I'm incredibly worried by it. If I had one primary wish for county cricket, it would be that every club focused as much on the mental side of the game as it does the physical and tactical. Fortunately, I know players who do take this issue very seriously and work with people who can support them. One of the best in the business is Hassan Khan of Consilium Leadership. I know Hass personally, and I've worked with him myself on a range of issues. I can't recommend him highly enough. When it comes to an understanding of how attitude and mindset can help high performance, there's no one better. He's a half-decent cricketer as well, as the boys at Finchley CC will know.

Despite the brilliant efforts of many people in the game, cricket is still in the dark ages when it comes to looking after the mental health and well-being of its players. Why clubs don't commit more resources to this area is utterly beyond me. I worry for many of the young cricketers coming into the game today precisely because of this lack of provision. They need to focus as much on their mental health as they do their physical health and the quality of their skills but they just don't have access to the resources to do it. I can't help but think that profit is being put before people at lots of clubs. But, of course, that way of thinking is utterly flawed because in business and in sport, your people are often your biggest asset. Their mental health and well-being have a direct impact on their performance and therefore their input. For too long now, organisations have treated the company's objectives and goals as something entirely different from the well-being of their employees. The two are inextricably and fundamentally linked and anyone that thinks differently belongs in the last century.

Leaders across cricket need to care about this issue much more than they do and take explicit, affirmative action to support players at all levels. Not doing so simply demonstrates a level of ignorance that could kill people. Cricket has one of the highest suicide rates of any sport and needs much more help on that front. Depression and anxiety always were, and still are, close at hand for me. When I left the game professionally, I promised myself that my career outside of cricket would give something back. I would try and make a difference in the lives of others. The only real hurdle in my mid-twenties was that I had no idea what success looked like outside of my cricket career. This lack of career advice is another common theme among young sportsmen and women, particularly given the increasingly fluid nature of the workplace. At least when I was 25, we knew what jobs might be roughly available to us in ten years. That's certainly not the case today.

As with many of these issues, the governing bodies have to be accountable and responsible for the welfare of the players and the sport they represent. If I'm honest, the Professional Cricketers' Association hasn't always been at the top of its game in this regard. A succession of pretty average CEOs hasn't helped. Having said that, the recent appointment of Rob Lynch as CEO is very good news for the game generally. I worked with Rob when he ran the commercial side at Middlesex and he's a good 'un. He's driven, he's highly competitive and he understands the game and the pathway given his own exploits as a young cricketer. Perhaps his two greatest assets are his energy and people skills. Both of these and the quality of the man himself suggest good times are ahead for the PCA.

A career that had initially promised much eventually found itself in the backyard of county cricket. It promised much because I had made my Middlesex club debut at 17 while still at Malvern College. I averaged 116 over 12 Test matches as an England Under-19 player in 1996/97, going on to be picked for the England A tour to Sri Lanka in 1998. That England A trip also allowed me to make my first property investment. It wouldn't be my last. My mum encouraged and helped me to find a flat. She's always been very smart when it comes to commercial opportunities and business generally. I bought a flat in Swan Walk in Shepperton using my £16,000 tour fee and then rented it out. The flat cost £130,000 and I sold it a few years later for £242,000. If there's one golden rule in life, it's that mums know best.

By 2006, the Middlesex management were fond of me but probably felt they could do better as my advancing years began to show. What then followed was a testimonial year that changed my life. For those of you not steeped in the world of bat and ball, clubs give cricketers a testimonial year to thank them for their contribution over many years. It supports events and fund-raising activities with the proceeds going to the cricketer who, in turn, donates some of those proceeds to charity. My testimonial year was the catalyst that led me to where I am now and the businesses we've built. It also allowed me to meet some fantastic people.

Andy Bowden from Coca-Cola was an amazing chairman of my testimonial committee. He went above and beyond for me on every level as did Simon Wakefield, Ian Milton and Karl Suntay at Sporting Index (the Chief to his mates) who were always there to pick me up and put a smile on my face when things were tough. They are great mates and I'll never forget the support they gave me.

Chief among the list of fantastic people involved was Paul Roy. Paul is a butcher's son from Epsom who, through sheer hard work, has had a glittering career. Merrill Lynch, NewSmith Capital and chairman of the British Horseracing Authority. Most recently, he's supported Sir Martin Sorrell's new company, S4 Capital, a disruptor in the marketing services sector. Sir Martin is a good guy too and loves his cricket.

I first met Paul while coaching his children. I was touched when, after the course, he called me up to say how much they had enjoyed it. In subsequent courses, he and his wife Sue came to watch and again, told me what a great job I was doing. At the time, as I was beginning my coaching courses, this meant a great deal. At that point, I had no idea what Paul did. I just knew he was a great bloke. I offered some of our subsequent sessions as a goodwill gesture, but he always sent me a (too generous) cheque afterwards. I guess in life, what goes around comes around.

Our friendship grew, and so it seemed natural for me to ask him to get involved in my benefit year. He agreed to become the patron, and he was simply amazing. At the opening dinner, he bought ten tables and donated over £30,000 of auction items. Even now, I'm still blown away by the generosity he showed. I still love the family today although Paul would say that I've got a funny way of showing it. We often play golf at Sunningdale or Queenwood, and during one of our visits, I had a shocker. A big duck hook left off the first tee straight into the back of his wife Sue's leg stood on the ladies' tee. I was mortified by it. Despite the bruise that my shit shot left, Sue did forgive me. I'm only glad Paul didn't see me play golf before our friendship blossomed. It could have been short-lived otherwise!

In my career, I had scored runs, made catches, and even taken wickets. I also have two first-class wickets to my name. My leg spin was often used as 'buffet bowling' when the opposition needed to rack up runs quickly to set us a target. One of my two wickets was that of Murray Goodwin, stumped by the Irish-Englishman Eoin Morgan. A wicket that was slightly called into question sometime later when I received a phone call from the ICC anti-corruption officer, Steve Richardson. He wanted to know if I knew anything about match-fixing concerning Murray Goodwin. After the call, I remember thinking how typical it was that one of my only two first-class wickets might have been a gimme. No case was ever proven against Murray, so those two wickets stand to this day. So, a 116 average, six wickets in six balls as a youngster and two first-class wickets. Little did I realise, at the time, how insignificant those stats were. What truly mattered to me were the people I had met along the way and the lessons l had learned on the field.

How much could these lessons apply to the business and the other ventures that I eventually set up? As often happens, we set our company up because we spotted a gap in the market as a result of my own experience. Thankfully, there was also a market in the gap. So D&G evolved, a business that has become such a defining part of my and my family's life today. Why D&G? I think it's fair to say that me and Glen didn't have much marketing magic back then. The D stood for David, and the G stood for Glen; genius!

Bails and Boardrooms is my story. The story of an ordinary boy from Sunbury, lightly blessed with a talent for hitting and catching a little red ball. It's the story of my business, my entrepreneurial zeal and the millions of pounds that we've raised for charity. It's a story of ambition, resilience, and determination coupled with personal struggle, but, above all, I hope it's a story that others will read and draw inspiration from. Anything is possible in life, providing that you're willing to listen, learn, roll with the punches, and work your nuts off.

Chapter Three

Life As A Classroom

ONE OF the great things about writing this book is that it's forced me to think about what matters to me, what I care about, and what has influenced me most. Surprisingly, chief among these is education, something that might astonish those who know me well. My own experience of the education system and much of what I've seen since tells me that everyone always asks the wrong question. 'How intelligent are you?' strikes me as an idiotic question to ask. I was never that good at school other than with things that interested me. That's true of most kids, right?

The Murtaghs have always played a big part in my life. At Malvern, Andrew Murtagh took on the unenviable task of guiding me through my later school years. He was chosen as my Housemaster given his own cricket career at Hampshire. He was also the man who, as my English teacher, spotted my first blatant bit of plagiarism. I never really recovered from that academically. As an aside, the second Mr Murtagh, his nephew Tim and my team-mate, was a marginally better bowler with much higher skin folds! In truth, I was really intelligent. I just didn't know how because no one ever asked the right question when I was younger.

'How are you intelligent?' would have been the jackpot question for two reasons. Firstly, because it assumes, rightly, that there are lots of different kinds of intelligence: emotional, social, physical, academic, musical, artistic and the rest. Secondly, that question doesn't prioritise academic knowledge above everything else. I've been able to progress in life not because I can write an essay about *Hamlet* or the causes of the First World War. It is because I've been able to get on with people everywhere. How well I can read a room of people and how well I've been able to put teams together and lead them. I did notice very early on in my life that people do buy people. It may sound a cliché, but it's one of the greatest truisms there is. I didn't learn those things in the classroom. I discovered them on the field of play, in the changing room, and with my team-mates. I also learned their importance from my parents, who, like me, have an excellent instinct for human connection. Thinking about it now, I'm not sure school taught me anything. Mind you, I keep that quiet in front of Jules when the kids are arguing about the pointlessness of homework.

What I have learned since, though, is the importance of doing what you know best, building on your strengths, and surrounding yourself with the very best people you can. The batsman who knows his scoring areas. The captain who knows his 'go-to' bowler at any moment. The coach who can get the very best out of everyone in the side. These people win matches. There's an old saying that first-rate people hire first-rate people and that second-rate people hire third-rate people. The then chairman of House of Fraser, Don McCarthy, taught me that and I will come back to more of his advice later. I've seen it in cricket, and I've seen it in business. The captain who wants to be centre stage. The batsman who can't celebrate other people's success when they fail. The boss who hires people who won't threaten them. It never works, and it eventually finds you out. I've been lucky in my later years to work out what I'm good at, and, crucially, I've found fantastic people who can help me make the most of these things. For that, I am genuinely grateful.

'Don't take yourself too seriously. No one else does.' That pretty much sums up my attitude on how to live life and, if Jules wouldn't leave me because of it, I would have it tattooed on my forehead.

I've always been that way, even in my cricketing days. I remember a great wind-up on Mohammad Ali. Mo joined Middlesex in 2006 as a left-arm quick. He became the bowler who we used to keep the ball rough on one side and dry to maximise reverse swing. In cricket as well, if you can make the seam of the ball more pronounced, you can get it to swing even further in unusual ways. Mo seemed to do that that better than most. In those days, we did it all the time although now, with cameras galore, you can't do it.

Mo had just taken six wickets in a game against Derbyshire. On the way back, I called him and pretended to be John Carr, one of the ECB big guns. I told Mo that his manipulation of the ball had gone too far and had been spotted that day on camera and asked if he could come to Lord's for a fingernail examination the next day. Silence ensued, followed by three words from Mo. 'Oh, bloody hell!' he said, immediately implicating himself. I just pissed myself down the phone. We loved a good wind-up in those days and I was better at it than most.

As I've never driven (Jules thinks it's because I can't reach the pedals), I was always in the passenger seat on the way home from games, keen to pass the time. I used to do a very good West Country accent and managed to reel in Nick Compton with it one day. Compo loved his cash and loved to have his massive ego stroked. So, I called him one day and pretended to be the Somerset director of cricket, Brian Rose. By the end of the call, I had Compo believing that Somerset were going to treble his wages on a five-year deal in one of the biggest transfers in cricketing history. He took the bait hook, line and sinker as he always did. Ironically, Compo ended up joining Somerset which was to be the catalyst for him living out his own dream of following in his grandfather Denis's footsteps by playing for England. I didn't envy Nick as I saw day to day the pressure that the Compton name put on him. I guess my way of trying to help him (and others where I could) was to keep the day to day things light and bright. Although he had a great career, I wish that Compo could have enjoyed it more for what it was. Every day seemed a battle for him as it sometimes was for me and I tried as much as I could to keep things enjoyable to help him put our great game in perspective.

The most engaging, most interesting people I've met in my life are the ones who work hard. They care about what they do but don't take themselves too seriously. Life's there for living and, as they say, you're a long time dead. On the rare occasion that I see a gravestone, I always notice that the sum parts of your life are a tiny dash between two dates. That's a scary thought, but it's always been a reminder for me that all of us are a pretty insignificant part of something much, much bigger. Realising that helps me not to take myself too seriously. Still, it also helps me put every day into perspective, something that I think isn't true for everyone. Some people do take themselves way too seriously. My middle name is Charles. It really ought to be Banter. It's my secret weapon, my greatest friend, and the thing that helps me keep life light-hearted. In fact, it was the only thing that got me a gig during the now infamous Stanford 20/20 tournament in the Caribbean. The captain, Shaun Udal (Shaggy to his mates), asked me to come along solely to do two things; boost team morale and look after the fines that would be issued for all manner of misdemeanours. I certainly wasn't getting a look in with the gloves given that Ben Scott was, by then, the established wicketkeeper. What a great role I had on that trip; right up my street.

I've discovered that when you start to think about writing a book, you begin to reflect on all sorts of things. One of the key things I've thought about is the people who matter most to me and why. I could name many, but I'll pick four for now. My grandad and his England schoolboy football caps played a big part in my young life. Showing them to my mates and reflecting on what he had achieved gave me the belief that perhaps one day, I, too, could be an elite sportsman. He died before I could get to know him well, but he's definitely at the top of the list of those who I'll buy a beer for in that bar in the sky that's waiting for all of us. Nelson Mandela is not someone you'd expect me to name in this list, but he's there. I first became aware of him on my England Under-15 tour to South Africa in 1992. That was a tour I'll never forget. To play with the likes of Flintoff, Tudor and Batty and be involved in a match-winning partnership with Freddie at Newlands was magical. That tour was the first time that I'd had to think about the relationship between sport and the outside world, and the impression made by one man's struggle against apartheid has stayed with me ever since. The underdog, the fighter, the great orator; the man Mandela was.

There are so many women in my life that a few of them were bound to make this list. Let me clarify that in case you wonder whether I'm a serial philanderer. I'm not. I have a mum, a wife, two stepdaughters and three daughters, so my life is not my own. My bathroom is certainly not my own, and it's safe to say I barely get a word in edgeways anywhere. That's not because they are women and I'm certainly not making a sweeping generalisation about how much women like to talk. It's merely down to the volume of them.

My daughters matter to me more than anything in the world, and they keep me sane. They make me smile every day even though I find them intensely frustrating at times. That's true of all dads, of course. They're only ever frustrating because they don't listen to me enough. They've taught me loads over the years. They've given me a reason to get up in the mornings, and some of them still laugh at my jokes. When you become a parent, you lose a massive amount of your natural selfishness, and I certainly have. You become a better person. The job is tough, and the business is stressful, but they always manage to keep my feet on the ground. To my five girls Lottie, Annabelle, Sophie, Emily and Leah – I just ask three things from you. Please be true to yourselves, treat others the way you'd like to be treated and be the best you can be every single day. I love you so much, girls.

The fourth and final addition to this list is probably the most professionally significant: Andrew John Strauss. Straussy. Sir Straussy. Or, my particular favourite nickname for him, which is SAS. Not my idea sadly but that of one of our mates, Mike O'Connor. Straussy was a man under whose leadership I am very proud to have played. Following the death of his amazing wife, Ruth, in 2018, the world witnessed the extraordinary way in which he handled her passing.

Straussy's work with the Ruth Strauss Foundation says all you need to know about him and his character. Selfless, full of grace, an outstanding communicator, and someone who is loved by all who know him. He would be the first to tell you that he wasn't the most naturally gifted cricketer, but he was the one with the most exceptional work ethic I have ever seen. One hundred Test matches and a double Ashes-winning captain before then going on to become the ECB's director of cricket and giving our game the leadership it so richly deserved. He was also the architect of the most magnificent World Cup win in history. It was his vision and leadership that began the journey that ended on that memorable day in July 2019. A genuinely outstanding career and a truly exceptional man. I could write an entire book about his impact on the way I now think. However, I've kept it to just my next chapter.

One of the things that I always say to my children is to be the very best version of themselves every day. At my best, I'd like to think that I'm exuberant, warm, a people person, a very embarrassing dad, and a family man at heart. I'd also like to think that I'm a risk-taker who can make things happen and that I've got an excellent eye for people. I've become pretty good at getting the deal done, and I've learned that you can't get anywhere in life if you don't take chances. The chapters that follow will, I hope, give you a flavour of what matters to me. Why and how I've used the lessons I've learned from cricket to become an entrepreneur and a better person. I've learned that leaders lead and the best ones lead by example and from the front. Cricket is a numbers game, and you can't hide behind your averages. The same is true for business. The old saying that 'revenue is vanity and profit is sanity' is never far from my mind. I've learned that finding ways of constantly measuring your success and reminding yourself of the numbers keeps everyone honest and on it. I've also learned that finding your real purpose in life is very hard, which is why I guess so few people manage to discover it. Once you do find your purpose, though, make sure you do everything to develop it, nurture it, and protect it.

Having a clear goal is one of life's great gifts. Understanding what culture is and how to build it has been one of the great lessons learned by the England cricket team, and I now know how much culture matters in business. Workplace culture is the single most significant factor for most people thinking about leaving an organisation. You can often tell what a company is like by the people they keep. In 2020, the real wages of work matter much more than money wages, and corporate well-being is at the very top of that list of real wages. As someone who has struggled with issues of mental well-being, this is something very close to my heart. Still, it's also an area that, I believe, offers a significant competitive advantage to any company that is genuinely willing to embrace its importance.

Finally, one of my most exceptional guides has always been my intuition. Over the years, I've learned to trust and respect the power of intuition. Some of the best captains I've seen have let heart rule head occasionally, and it's paid huge dividends. Many of the opportunities I've missed in my life have been because I haven't trusted my gut instinct. My gut instinct told me to write this book. I hope I was right.

Chapter Four

A Fish Rots from its Head

AS THE ancient Chinese proverb tells us, 'a fish rots from the head'. It's not strictly true of course (I think it's the stomach first). Still, there have been enough corporate scandals and abject company failures in recent years to highlight the essence of that proverb. We're living through unprecedented times politically and socially. As I write this book, I can't help but look back at the raft of so-called leaders who tried to plot the country's way through the European maze last year and wonder how many rotting heads there were in charge of that debate. I hope Nigel Farage doesn't come after me for that one.

Over many years in cricket and business, I've come to realise that teams and organisations succeed because they have leaders who have the right values. The leaders communicate those values powerfully and stand by them every day. Great leaders lead from the front and not the back. The clue is, after all, in the title. I have to be honest and say that I don't read very many business books. Still, one which had a profound effect on me some years ago was Simon Sinek's brilliant and insightful book, *Start with Why*. In it, he argues the case for why every business in the world should ask itself the question, 'Why do we exist?' Of course, it seems obvious when you think about it. What is your company's real reason for being? The mistake many businesses make, of course, is to focus on the what, not the why. The train company which talks about how it gets passengers from A to B. In other words, what it does, rather than celebrating the part it plays in bringing people together. In other words, why it does it. The technology company focusing on the power of its artificial intelligence engine rather than the world of possibilities it opens up for people. Or, closer to home, the cricket club which focuses solely on the number of games it wants to win rather than on how it wants to win matches. Or, how it nurtures a generation of young cricketers who live the right values and play the right way.

Middlesex are winners in this regard as is one of my other great pals in cricket, big Gus Fraser. If you cut that man, he bleeds Middlesex. You won't meet anyone in the game with a clearer set of values and beliefs about how to do the right things. Those values and beliefs were tested a couple of years ago during the now infamous 'bow and arrow' incident at the Oval.

An arrow, fired on to the outfield, stopped play and prevented Middlesex from declaring and bowling again to correct their over-rate. Without being able to do that, Middlesex would have lost two points. In the melee of that afternoon's madness, Gus wanted clarification from the umpires that the stoppage wouldn't mean docked points for a slow over-rate. He received this clarification from the umpires and so agreed to come off. As is now well known, the ECB docked the two points, and just a single point relegated Middlesex. Gus was furious, the club was beside itself, and the club considered legal action. In the end, the respect Gus has for the game mattered more, and no further action was taken.

I know it's still a very sore point with Gus, but life moves on for all of us. As an aside, I think Straussy got it very wrong that day. His view was that the points should have been deducted because it was impossible to know how the game would have panned out. Respect him immensely though I do, I don't think that was Straussy's finest hour. Perhaps his corporate-self got the better of him on that occasion. Gus has been a friend, mentor and teacher for many years now. He was a fantastic cricketer, and he is an even better bloke. Like all of us, though, he has areas to develop in his abilities as a leader, but I hope he plays a significant role in the future of Middlesex for years to come. As a county, we need to get better at identifying the players we want moving forward. If they are elsewhere, we need to work harder and earlier to persuade them that Lord's is their home. Gus has a big part to play in this, and hopefully, Middlesex will get better at it.

Having a purpose matters, and this is something I'll come back to later in the book. This sense of purpose means that every morning I get out of bed to try to give something back. Work is more than just about earning money, looking after my family and keeping me out of trouble; it's a chance to make a difference. I passionately believe this, and our teams do all they can to live this vision. We judge ourselves by how much of a difference we're making. I hope it will be a long time before we have the smell of rotting fish in our office.

One of the leaders I have come to admire most in my life is Penny Hughes. Penny's career reads like a who's who of the business world. Proctor & Gamble, Coca-Cola, Vodafone, RBS and Trinity Mirror to name but a few. She was also the first female chairman at Aston Martin. Before that and at the ripe old age of 33, Penny became president of the UK and Ireland businesses of Coca-Cola for an excellent reason. She's fearless, has a considerable depth of knowledge and insight and combines this with ambition, steel and drive in abundance. 'Sometimes, it is better not to know everything, just to know enough. You can then bring in fresh ideas,' she once said to me. How true that is, and I've taken it upon myself to make sure that I never try to know everything. In my case, that's more by accident than design! One of Penny's most significant achievements has been to manage a brilliant career at the same time as raising two fantastic sons, Alex and Robbie. It's something I've watched with huge admiration over the years and which has helped me understand the importance of achieving the right balance. I'm fortunate to know people like Penny. I'll never forget how vital a role she played on my benefit committee, nor the way she conducted herself during that period. She has taught me so much.

The world of sport is full of examples, good and bad, of the real power of leadership. In football, if you want to build something for the long term, your first call might not be to José Mourinho. He's a brilliant leader to give you short-term, immediate impact. If you want to get the very best out of what you have, you might call Jürgen Klopp. Or, if your back is up against the wall, there's a chap called Sam Allardyce whose number you might need. All leaders in their own way and with their strengths and weaknesses. Different leaders for different times and different situations. Very few are the complete package with the skills and temperament to lead in all sorts of different circumstances. The most complete leader I have ever come across is Andrew Strauss. My respect and admiration for him knows no bounds. I would like to focus now on what I believe made and makes him very special as a leader. He has been possibly the most significant influence on my career, both in terms of what I do but also how I do it, so let's look at how he shaped his extraordinary leadership skills.

In 2009 English cricket was not in good shape. That's putting it mildly. The new England captain, Straussy himself, walked into a dressing room which was riven by tensions and divisions. It's possible to read a significant number of articles about that period in the game. No further commentary from me could add to what's already out there. I may, however, offer a couple of brief observations later about a certain cricketer called Kevin Pietersen.

Straussy's first press conference was very significant for two reasons. Firstly, because he needed to make his mark quickly. Secondly, because he also knew it was an opportunity for him to signal change: the message, his demeanour and his interaction with and management of the media needed to be perfect. With the confidence and innate skill of the brilliant opening batsman that he was, he nailed it, of course. Every question deftly handled, and every topic played with a straight bat. What particularly struck me as I watched his performance at that press conference was how important it was that he made the right first impression. He also needed to set the correct tone for his leadership. It's a lesson that has stayed with me since that day. First impressions matter and you've only got one opportunity to set out your stall and make that first impression. Take that opportunity, and the journey suddenly becomes a little easier. That lesson has stayed with me ever since and guided my approach in countless new business presentations and meetings, both formal and informal.

The world consists of two types of people, and you can tell in which category the person you are talking to belongs within about 90 seconds. Some people inspire, enthuse, engage, move forwards and exude a positive intent in all they do. I call those people radiators, and it's a type I know well because, according to most who know me, I am one. I love spending time with and being around radiators. They energise, excite and stimulate and are great fun. They give out an infectious energy.

There are others in the world who, even before they have opened their mouths to speak, have somehow made everyone around them feel worse about themselves. I call these people drains, and I try to avoid them like the plague. They are the mood hoovers of life.Sadly, I know a few in both business and in cricket. Phil Neale, for example, the current England operations manager, has it in him to be an entire sewage farm at times. Phil was my England under 19 team manager and that was definitely my experience of him on tour. At a time when the lads often needed a 'lift' having been away for a while, Phil was definitely not the man for that job! When Straussy took the England job, he encouraged everyone, including the drains, to air their feelings and problems openly and honestly in a closed-door session. It would have been easy to ignore or dismiss the drains (too cynical, too miserable, not team players) but Straussy chose not to do that. He insisted that nobody left anything in the locker. Negative baggage jettisoned and a fresh start. As a leader, Straussy knew that negativity in his team was going to get in the way of almost everything he wanted to achieve, so he met the problem head-on. Good leaders lead from the front, and they do so with transparency and honesty. It's a key lesson I've learned, and it's how I've tried to build my business since day one. I can think of a few county dressing rooms over the years that would have been far happier places with his kind of approach.

In the famous words of one Ricky Gervais, 'There is no i in "team".' However, if you look hard enough, there is, of course, a 'me'. The dynamic of how to build a real team ethos can only ever be crafted by a leader who understands that the team must come before any 'me', including themselves. Straussy created an environment in the England squad in which star players knew that their performances mattered but not as much as the team's effort. The 'Principles Charter', which he encouraged the players to create, was another mark of a man leading from the front. The charter defined how the team saw itself, how it should behave, and what standards every member of the group needed to achieve. It was a move of real genius to create a shared agenda driven by the players. Australia and, in particular, Cameron Bancroft, must have wished for a charter like this moments after his nether regions were being roughed up by a piece of sandpaper.

To be fair, this process of building a team applies to almost anything you do with a group of people; everyday leadership if you like. My own recent house project through Elston Developments was a great reminder of how important it is to have a bunch of people who work together despite being from different disciplines. All of the usual leadership rules applied; a clear set of objectives, good communication and a shared goal. The only real difference was that Jules was the leader in this project, not me. No wonder we finished the build on time and on budget!

The film *Parenthood* is one of my favourites. In it, Steve Martin utters the immortal line: 'Some people have a way with words. Some not have way.' Straussy most definitely has the gift of the gab, and he uses it brilliantly to sell his decisions with confidence and conviction. The most important thing to learn here is that it's not just the way that you communicate your decisions when you are confident that you are right. Possibly even more important is how you choose to communicate when you just cannot be sure that you've made the right decision. Leadership sometimes involves dealing with the unknown and the uncertain. As I added the final touches to this book, the coronavirus pandemic was at its peak. The unknowns are currently a massively testing time for global leaders everywhere. Communicating any decision and desired direction with commitment and total clarity will be more persuasive and so likely to get much more buy-in. Again, the art of real leadership is making a decision and making sure that people know you think that it's the right decision. Leaders with conviction carry teams with them in a way that others don't.

Perhaps the most important lesson I learned from Straussy, though, wasn't about the action of how to lead but more the power of being able to delegate. There have been times when I have felt overwhelmed in my business life at the sheer number and weight of decisions I'm making and the number of factors involved in those decisions. I now know that the best leaders have the guts and the confidence to delegate in those situations and to leave themselves free to focus on the next destination for their business. Straussy did that in spades and still does. If, as a leader, you surround yourself with brilliant people who can help you by doing the things that you are less good at, it's tough to fail. In my experience, most people are much better than they think they are and, given a chance to shine, they take the opportunity with both hands. I love seeing people, young and old, thrive because they've been encouraged to ask for forgiveness and not permission in the decisions they make. Employ the best people, believe and trust in their potential, and they will rise to the challenge.

According to Google's advanced algorithms, at the time of writing this book, there were nearly 190 million books in circulation around the world. I guess about 185 million of those books (perhaps a slight exaggeration) revolve around leadership of some sort, so I did approach this chapter with some trepidation. That was until I realised that some of my stories involved bacon, chocolate, booze and drains. Not many other leadership books seem to reference these! Hence, I thought I might be able to cut through the sea of dull advice out there with the help of these subjects and the cast of colourful characters in those stories. At this point in the book, I need to add a couple of important caveats. According to Jules, I'm a lovely man who believes the world is full of great people who always do the right thing. However, I've discovered over the years that this isn't always the case. This has taught me some other very valuable leadership lessons, which I thought I would share at this point in our journey together.

I once played under a Middlesex captain called Mike whom I hero-worshipped growing up. In many ways, I still do. Sadly, I never played under the legend that was Mr Brearley, so it was the other one, and his surname wasn't Atherton. That man did like a bacon sandwich and still does. Sadly, your heroes sometimes let you down. I'll never forget the day that Mike Gatting was yelling at us during a bleep test while filling his face with his favourite sandwich. Or the night on our pre-season tour to South Africa where he tried to give us a team talk on one-day strategy. He was in his hotel room with us. The only difference was that he was wearing nothing but a towel round his waist and the Spaghetti Bolognese on his hairy chest from the room service he had just ordered.That evening was actually cut short because Gatt had to leave us to head out on the lash with a mate. These are all images which have stayed with me for years because I vividly remember how wrong I thought that behaviour was. On those days, I guess I realised that even your heroes are flawed. Those moments helped me hugely in my business career as it happens. I never ask any of my teams to do something I'm not prepared to do myself. Or, to put it another way, I try not to piss on someone's shoe while telling them it's raining. Never a good look in sport or business.

There is a widespread view that most leaders are psychopaths and well-respected studies do demonstrate the link between psychopathy and leadership. Those studies may well be spot on, but I suspect from experience that most great leaders aren't psychopaths. They are the very opposite. Selfless, emotionally intelligent, ego-free and focused entirely on the greater good of the company or team's purpose and the people delivering it. And that's why a fantastically talented cricketer called Kevin could never have led England or, for that matter any other country, to glory. As the saying goes: 'If he were made of chocolate, he would have eaten himself.' Again, behaviour that is the very antithesis of what makes for great leadership. A fantastic cricketer but someone who always saw the 'me' in team and so no leader of men (or women) sadly.

To be fair, I spotted KP's character very early. He got a brilliant 170 for Notts against us in his early days. It was the first time I'd seen him bat and it was like nothing I'd seen before. His array of shots and confidence was incredible. Tuffers, bowling over the wicket into day three rough, was being dispatched over extra cover with ease. I decided to get stuck into him early with a bit of sledging. Instead of merely ignoring my abuse, KP immediately marched to the square-leg umpire and demanded that I stopped. The insult I kept using was 'doos'. This is a book for young and old, so I won't translate it here. Suffice to say, it's not pleasant. It was, however, accurate. I was a good judge of character. Years later, I'll never forget KP's lack of interest, support or enthusiasm for my benefit year even though I was only asking him to sign a few bats. His selfishness at that time stood out, given the unbelievable support I had received from everyone else in the game. It taught me a great deal about the man at that stage in his life. I'm delighted to see that he is now doing all he can to support conservation projects in his homeland. That's a great thing to do and a great effort from him. With age comes wisdom and selflessness, I guess.

I experienced that kind of selflessness very unexpectedly from the great Shane Warne. During my benefit year, we played against Hampshire. While I was in the nets practising, Warney was watching intently from the other end, which struck me as a bit odd. Not least because he only needed to see me play one ball to work out how to get me out! At the end of the net session, he stopped me to explain that he'd heard it was my benefit year and that I was exactly the kind of bloke that benefit years were designed for; loyal servants of one club. He then went on to offer as many signed items as I wanted for my auctions. I think, in the end, we had 59 items signed by him. I was hugely touched and honoured that one of the greats of the game had taken the time to seek me out and help me out. Warney was, and still is, a champion human being.

My final food and beverage-based observation on leadership would be a much broader one. Leaders craft visions but they crucially also build cultures. Witness what Straussy did to the England squad. Most great leaders I've ever met understand that culture starts with people. A team that drinks together stays together. What do I mean by that? Cricket, business and life can be highly stressful and create significant pressure on the individual. An opportunity for drinking downtime (with or without alcohol) gives people time to reflect and discuss things with team-mates and to leave behind the potential disappointment from the day. It's a time for critical reflection and an opportunity to remind yourself that it's only a game, a deal or a meeting. Another one will come along next week, and no one has died. The opposite is also true, of course. Success needs celebrating, and teams should enjoy the good times. There's almost no point in winning otherwise.

The second reason I believe that the opportunity to be together socially matters for any organisation's culture is because this creates the chance to celebrate other people's success. I would argue that this is not just an essential part of creating a positive and productive culture but vital in sport and business. Over the years, I've met too many people for whom a little piece of them dies when someone else succeeds. Allowing this to happen creates a genuinely toxic culture and can lead to poor mental health and distress. If I could, I'd tell every young cricketer entering the professional game today, this one golden rule: celebrate other people's success. You will find yourself happier, less focused on your performance, more popular and ultimately more successful. In one of those 185 million books on leadership I mentioned, this is defined as having a growth mindset. In my world, it's described as being a good bloke.

Finally, and most importantly, the social aspect of any culture you build as a leader allows your team to meet new people and to talk about new things. This social aspect is the very lifeblood of the ecosystem in which we all thrive, whether it be in the world of sport or business. As Socrates

– the Greek philosopher, not the great Brazilian footballer – once said, 'Weak minds discuss people, average minds discuss events, but great minds discuss ideas.' Talking about ideas stimulates people and, as a leader, you want your people to be engaged, excited and creative. So, there you are; bacon, chocolate, booze and drains as start points for valuable leadership lessons. Eat your heart out, Simon Sinek. Nashy is coming for you!

I started this chapter on leadership with the best sporting leader I've been lucky enough to know. I couldn't finish without reference to two of the very best CEOs I've ever worked with in my business life. Leadership from the front is essential. So is the role that a leader has in building the right sort of culture for an organisation. I saw this in cricket with Straussy and in the world of business very clearly through John King at House of Fraser and Nick Beighton at ASOS. Both men worked together in their early days, and both have had an enormous influence on my life. John King is a leader in every sense of the word. As CEO at House of Fraser, along with Nigel Oddy and Simon Duncan, he did something I'll never forget which is to give our business its first break. In our first meeting, I'd asked him to give us a chance in the same way that someone had probably given him his first chance once. It's something I believe passionately to this day. Everyone needs their first break and first opportunity to impress and John certainly gave us that. 'We've got to go big, mate,' may be the best brief I've ever had but they were also the words that allowed our business to be born. John wanted his company to do all it could to support its charity ambitions and build a compelling strategy for their corporate social responsibility. We were fortunate that he trusted us to do this. Some years later, John told me that I reminded him of himself in business. I was hugely flattered at the time (and still am) but looking back, I think he was right. Both of us do all we can to go the extra mile, and both of us work very hard. John's evident and practical view of the business world mirrored that of the All Blacks. No dickheads. It's something that has stayed with me throughout my business life. That period also taught me the real value of nurturing your friendships and relationships. John King, Nigel Oddy and Simon Duncan have all been incredibly good to me over the years and their support and friendship is something that I'll never forget. All three of them know that what goes around comes around and that, whatever happens in the future, I'm there for all of them come rain or shine.

In Nigel's case, I'm actually lucky that he's still talking to me. Some years ago, we all attended John Caudwell's annual fundraiser. Nigel had just come back from China and as a result of sheer fatigue, nodded off during the auction. I suggested to a couple of my colleagues that it would be fun to wind Nigel up with a bid that never happened. Little did I know that my team would take me up on it. The next day, I received a call from Nigel who, himself, had received a beautifully mocked-up invoice from the event organisers for £60,000. Of course, it hadn't come from them at all. My team had done it themselves and sent it as a wind-up. Needless to say, Nigel went into a tailspin and called John Caudwell himself, only to be told that the invoice looked like it had been sent from our company, D&G. As ever with Nigel, he saw the funny side.

Nick Beighton is a man who leads from the front and for whom culture is also crucial. ASOS doesn't do hierarchy, and you'll often find the directors hot desking along with everyone else. Nick and his executive team speak to everyone at their regular new starter breakfast meetings. In those meetings, new starters are encouraged to be themselves, and they regularly discuss the things that are important to ASOS. As a leader, he walks the walk and doesn't just talk the talk. ASOS celebrates doing things differently, and this includes making sure that no new starter joins on a Monday because everyone hates that day of the week. It's a small touch from a big-thinking CEO who instinctively knows what leadership is and how important it is to build the team ethos. We've always felt important to ASOS, despite our lack of importance to their day-to-day operations. That alone is a testament to Nick's qualities as a leader. He's a man from whom I've learned a great deal.

In a chapter on leadership in which the stench of rotting fish, Sam Allardyce, chocolate, bacon and psychopaths have all featured, I would like to give the last word to Straussy. Let's end on a final leadership lesson from him that I've probably used more than any of the others both with my team and my clients: don't let other people do the dirty work. Straussy learned this lesson the hard way having dropped Steve Harmison from the Test team, only to let Andy Flower break the bad news. I know it's something he regrets to this day, but sometimes your mistakes can be your most significant lessons. If you are giving bad news or telling someone you've made a mistake, then look them directly in the eye when you do so. Everyone has their perspective, and everyone sees things very differently. This insight is essential when you're telling someone that they've missed out on an opportunity or, worse still, that they aren't performing. Even in those situations, make that person feel valued by offering ways to improve or ideas to develop their skills elsewhere. They may still want to express their frustration, anger or disappointment. If that's the case, let them because it may be better for them to do it with you than with other people. In the end, good leaders set their stall out by leading from the front. They are responsible for building the right culture, choosing the right people and finding the right path to success. Most importantly, if they do all of those things in the most human way possible, they will have a shot at being genuinely top class at what they do.

Chapter Five

The Best Things Come in Small Packages

AND I should know!

During my cricket career, I wish I'd known that the little things truly mattered. Not just because commentators and journos described me as diminutive but because, as I now know, cricket is a game built on small margins. The bat you use, the gloves you wear, the routine you have before a match. These matter much more than the ludicrous superstitions I used to have while playing cricket. Where I walked, what I touched and what I did before and during a game were all part of a bizarre ritual for me.

Or, at least I thought it was a bizarre ritual. Recently, a period of cognitive behavioural therapy taught me otherwise.

My anxiety and these superstitions were and are all linked to my mental well-being. Odd though it may seem to anyone who doesn't suffer this, the many superstitions I had were all linked to me believing that bad things would happen if I didn't do these things. The tree I walked past and needed to touch in case someone died if I didn't. The stumps I needed to walk round three times in case I dropped a catch and let the lads down. Or having to make sure our front doormat was perfectly straight when I left home in case I nicked off early. Looking back now, I was a mess. Many of my worries revolved around profound life and death thoughts, all linked to my mental health. It's one of the reasons I've worked so hard to understand my own state of mind and my own anxieties over the years. It's still a work in progress if I'm honest but aren't we all? I guess some of us are just slightly more challenged than others.

Clearly none of my odd behaviour had anything to do with the real marginal gains that help peak performance. I had no idea as a cricketer how understanding these marginal gains could translate into building a business. As the saying goes, 'the best way to eat an elephant is one tiny chunk at a time'. Our company has thrived over the last few years because we've focused on making sure that we make the little everyday things our key priority. Having a vision and a strategy matter hugely, but concentrating on the detail of how you execute that strategy and improving what you do every day is the real foundation of success. Enter *kaizen*, a concept that neatly sums up this way of thinking. Having discovered it early in my business life, it is now one of my guiding hands in life and business.

If someone had asked me what *kaizen* meant when I was younger, I dread to think what kind of answers I'd have given. I didn't spend too much time thinking about strategic frameworks, business philosophies and the Japanese language when I was at the crease or in the changing room. I wish that I had because if the concept of *kaizen* been an ever-present one in my life as a professional cricketer, I might have done better. I also had no idea how much this idea would come to help me build my business for the long term. More importantly, it has given me a blueprint for how I approach so many of life's challenges.

First, here is an explanation. *Kaizen* originated in Japan, and the word translated means change (*kai*) for the better (*zen*). It's an approach which focuses on the philosophical belief that everything (and I'd argue everyone) can be improved. Some organisations and teams look at their processes and complacently think that everything is fine. We all know a few of those. *Kaizen* demands something very different. It believes that every process can be improved and that nothing is the status quo. Continuous efforts can improve everything and can result in small, often imperceptible changes over time. These incremental changes add up to substantial changes over the long term which, in turn, enhance performance across the board. That's the theory anyway, and *kaizen* is one way of putting it. Creating marginal gains is another.

What does this mean then in practice for sport, people and business? Well, let's start with an interesting story and follow that with looking at the science of cricket in detail to help us understand why marginal gains in that sport matter so much. The story is from the world of hockey, which is another sport involving a small ball whacked around at pace. As far back as Athens in 2004, GB weren't good enough to even send a women's hockey team to the Olympics let alone challenge for a medal. By 2008, Beijing was better, and we won a bronze in 2012. Things changed after that, sadly. The coach left with damaging consequences, and at the World Cup in 2014, the team came 11th. Rio was only two years away by then, and this was a team on a downward spiral for whom any sort of medal was a distant dream.

Team GB's 'marginal gain' plan managed to change all that. I wonder whether they knew the Japanese called it *kaizen*. That 'marginal gain' plan became the team's blueprint for success, and it worked a treat. They looked at everything they needed to do to win gold and broke it down into tiny chunks. They examined every process and every feature of their team to find those marginal gains. They designed a whole new fitness plan, but it wasn't the plan that was the game-changer. It was how they approached the plan.

Every day in the past, the team would turn up at the exact start time of a session. Jackets off, headphones off, a few quick hellos and already ten minutes had passed. They decided that this was not good enough in a professional environment. By changing their routine and turning up ten minutes early to get those things done, they gained an extra 42 hours of training time a year. That's what you call a very significant marginal gain. They also worked out how to improve their attitude before each game. Not with a world-renowned sports psychologist. They changed where they sat on the way to a game. Previously, the seating had been a free-for-all. Now they worked out who liked a quiet space, who wanted to chat, who loved listening to music and they sat them next to each other. The net result was that the team arrived at the game happier, more relaxed and better prepared. Again, a marginal gain that made a big difference.

Marginal gains in hand, they headed to the 2016 Olympics and eventually the final. It turned out to be the match of their lives, but an even bigger test was around the corner. A penalty shoot-out. The ultimate test of the marginal gain plan. The team became Olympic champions in a dramatic finish. I've often wondered if they used the extra 42 hours they found for training on penalties. I love that story because it tells you all you need to know about the world of sport. If you commit yourself to making lots of tiny improvements, you really can achieve anything, even a gold medal.

Cricket, as many people will know reading this book, is a funny old game. Bob Woolmer once summed up the relative absurdity of what I used to do for a living by explaining that, 'to review the raw, split-second data of what happens when a player executes a shot is to wonder how anyone survives more than one delivery'.

Of course, he's right, and it was a thought that crossed my mind once or twice a day when I was playing. The equipment we use in the game is equally odd. The bat is about 38 inches in length and 4½ inches wide, weighing anything between 2lb 6oz and over 3lb. One bat, one ball and 22 yards between them. No wonder so many people find it weird. It's dangerous too, and while the horrific and devastating death of my brilliant ex-team-mate and friend Phillip Hughes in November 2014 was a tragic one-off, cricket is a dangerous sport. The West Indian batsman, Gordon Greenidge, was once hit so violently in the nether regions that his box split in two and he was stretchered off to the dressing room, vomiting. I've got a few eye-watering memories myself although I guess I was lucky to have a smaller target in that area for bowlers to aim at!

The science of cricket tells you why the small things do make a big difference. 'Watch the ball' is one of the most common things coaches say to youngsters. It was Justin Langer's signature piece of advice during his stint as captain at Middlesex. He would always say that providing you watched the ball closely enough, it was impossible to get out. 'Easy for someone of your ability to say that,' I used to think when he offered those words of wisdom to me. I noticed in the recent brilliant Amazon Prime series *The Test* that Langer still has that advice in his locker. Funnily enough, I must have missed the episode in which he gave the Aussies the other piece of advice he always used to provide us with. Needless to say that advice involved how 'good looking chicks' (his words) responded to men who are winners. You can probably work out the rhyme yourself. Thank God that the world has moved on from some of the things I used to hear in the dressing room. That dodgy bit of advice aside, the Australian cricket team is in great hands with Langer at the helm. He's very tough, no-nonsense and a born winner; great qualities to have for any leader.

So, 'watching the ball' is excellent advice, but we now know what that looks like. In his superb book *The Meaning of Cricket*, Jon Hotten explains how Michael Land and Peter McLeod expanded on the already existing research. How a batsman responds when facing a delivery and what they discovered was fascinating. As the ball leaves the bowler's hand, a batsman's head is still and watching the ball. Just 140 milliseconds later, the eyes are rapidly moving downwards to where the batsman thinks the ball will pitch. As the ball bounces, the eyes re-engage with the ball. The net result of which is that the eyes are only on the ball for 57% of its 600-millisecond journey. The rest of the time is about instinct, flair and anticipation.

Why on earth would you walk us through all of these boring scientific stats, Nashy? One good reason. Given this statistical and scientific backdrop, it's fair to say that cricket is a game made for marginal gains (or *kaizen* as I like to say). Andy Flower instinctively knew this too. His England side were intense in their preparation and not just around the obvious skills. They wanted to identify who produced the least amount of sweat during a game. In doing so, they could put this individual in charge of keeping the ball dry in the field; a critical part of getting the ball to reverse swing. So, fitness tests followed and one of the fittest players in the group, Alastair Cook, was shown to be the man that sweated least of all. From that point on, England used him to significant effect to achieve a much higher percentage of reverse swing in critical series, including our memorable win Down Under. In that series alone, England made the ball reverse 13 overs earlier than the Aussies. There's a magnificent example of a marginal gain.

The more precise the sport is the more *kaizen* matters. The smaller the margin of error, the more significant difference focusing on minor improvements will make. I spent an entire cricket career living with that concept every day, but it's only in the last few years that I've been able to understand it. What a stinker! As a batsman, tiny changes to the way you set up as you face the bowler can make a huge difference. In my playing days, I knew that. I just didn't realise how big a difference that concept would make to my life in business.

For that reason, county cricketers today need to commit themselves to as many marginal gains as possible. Here are a few unexpected ones from me and a few from players marginally more famous than me.

Young people have no idea how important sleep is. People perform better on optimum levels of sleep. In particular, young batsmen have no idea how important sleep is for them. It's a marginal gain jackpot because an hour's extra sleep at night means everything during those milliseconds watching that ball: more significant focus, greater anticipation and quicker reactions. If you need any more convincing, read *Why We Sleep* by Matthew Walker. It will change the way you think about the importance of sleep forever.

As an aside, I worry about my children's generation. Screens, lack of sleep and too much focus on the immediate gratification of a 'like' on social media. I hate social media. Why would you spend your life looking at other people's lives when you could spend that time enjoying your own? It's madness. One of the many reasons that I still love watching the game of cricket after all these years is that the most prolonged form of the game is the ultimate antidote to modern life. It's slow, it's highly nuanced, and it takes time to understand it. I love it now because I have a beer rather than a bat in hand. To get back to my original point, any young county batsmen reading this, get more sleep! It will give you an edge on and off the field.

Here's another marginal gain that the followers of *kaizen* would love. Riddle me this. A professional batsman needs around three to six hours to make a century. A session of cricket typically lasts two hours during a game. Yet, time and time again, I see batsmen practising in 20- to 30-minute chunks in the nets. It drives me mad. They are training their brains to bat for no longer than half an hour so they shouldn't be surprised if they only bat for that length of time in a match. If you want to score big runs and bat for a long time, you have to practise that way too. Get into the nets for hours at a time. You'll eventually learn to bat that way.

The great Australian batsman, Ricky Ponting, understood *kaizen* although I'm not sure he spoke Japanese. He insisted that all of the Australian fast bowlers use new balls at him in the nets because that's what he'd face most often in a game situation. To watch him practising before a game told you that he loved a marginal gain. Where all of the other players would practise hitting the ball back past the thrower, he would deliberately play practice shots to all angles, working his bat face to best replicate the kind of shots he wanted to hit in the game. Not unsurprisingly, Ricky Ponting was one of the finest players ever to grace the world stage.

Looking back on my career, I've known a few players and coaches to actively embrace *kaizen*, even if they didn't know its origins. One of the shortest coaching reigns at Middlesex was that of Richard Pybus. Appointed in February 2007, he left the club in July of the same year. He had some fascinating ideas, but it's fair to say that they weren't universally embraced. The intent was right, however. He wanted to find ways for us to make marginal gains, including relaxing the afternoon before games with our pillows from home lying on the floor listening to his meditation tapes. I remember one session in Swansea seeing Owais Shah lying next to me. He rolled his eyes and whispered, 'How the f*** is this going to get me a ton tomorrow, dog?' I guess Richard might have been ahead of his time from our point of view. In

2009, he became the South African coach of the year, having rejoined the Titans in South Africa after leaving us. Perhaps those pillows worked slightly better in warmer climes.

I've just mentioned Owais Shah, so I'm going to afford myself the luxury of a quick digression. Owais was, by some considerable margin, the most naturally gifted batsman I ever played with. He was unbelievable; 80 on his international debut. The closest we have to a player like Owais in the England set-up at the moment is Ollie Pope. Natural talent in abundance and fearless with it. From the looks of how Ollie carries himself, he seems very good at 'playing the game'. The right words about the right people at the right time.

That's where the comparison with Owais ends, sadly. If Owais had demonstrated any ability to 'play the game', he may have gone on to be one of England's most successful batsmen. He didn't 'play the game' and, as a result, he limited his international career significantly. Straussy and Duncan Fletcher were never able to get the best out of Owais. I don't know to this day whether that's because Owais was a totally different character to most of the dressing room at the time or whether there was something more sinister going on. The likes of Jones,Trescothick and Collingwood all shared the same work ethic and demeanour. It was true that Owais could be divisive and perceived as selfish and aloof but he was a gun player. I believe passionately that leadership is not about managing people who toe the line. It's about getting the very best out of the people who perform best, even if some of those people represent a management challenge.

I knew the writing was on the wall for Owais when he told me that Fletcher had ignored him for almost his whole debut tour. Worse still, Fletcher found it impossible to even make eye contact with Owais in the hotel. At the time, I didn't think that it was a recipe for a happy cricketing marriage and sadly I was right.

I'm still gutted to this day about the way Owais was treated because he is one of my great mates. On the subject of mates, this is probably a good time to mention my cricketing pals in general. To all of you and you know who you are. It's been the joy of my life to spend time playing and drinking with you all. I guess there's an excellent reason why some of our stories didn't make the pages of this book! Thanks for everything you've done to support me over the years. It has meant the world to me, and I hope, likewise, you've always felt that you can count on my support too. Life's a two-way street, and there's no more significant evidence of that than in the sporting world amongst friends.

Now, back to our marginal gains. At the Rio Olympics, every member of the 14-strong cycling track team won a medal. Were they fitter? Were they technically better? Did they have better equipment? Not quite. The answer lies again, partly, in *kaizen*. British Cycling's performance director, Sir Dave Brailsford, summed it up perfectly when he said, 'Forget about perfection, focus on progression, and compound the improvements.' Speaking to the *Harvard Business Review* in 2015, Brailsford explained:

> By experimenting in a wind tunnel, we searched for small improvements to aerodynamics. By analysing the mechanics' area in the team truck, we discovered that dust was accumulating on the floor, undermining bike maintenance. So, we painted the floor white, to spot any impurities. We hired a surgeon to teach our athletes about proper handwashing to avoid illnesses during competitions (we also decided not to shake any hands during the Olympics). We were precise about food preparation. We brought mattresses and pillows so our athletes

> could sleep in the same posture every night. We searched for small improvements everywhere and found countless opportunities. Taken together, we felt they gave us a competitive advantage.

That's an impressive list of marginal gains, and it's hardly surprising that we've dominated cycling for so long. The exciting thing for me about that list is also how creatively they've managed to solve the problems. Clearly, a considerable amount of time and effort went into finding the solutions as well as identifying the issues.

Kaizen in sport makes a massive difference although few, if any sportsmen or women, may know it as that. I've learned over the years how important it is in business, too. Not unsurprisingly given its Japanese heritage, Toyota is one of the very best examples of *kaizen* in action in business. Since the end of World War Two, Toyota's production system has extolled the virtues of what they call 'lean manufacturing'. It sounds quite dull and it probably is for most people, but it's key to how you improve your company's output. It's the process by which, through the complete elimination of waste, inconsistencies and unreasonable requirements on the production line, quality products happen. All of these notions are central to the *kaizen* philosophy. They can be very well applied in the manufacturing environment.

Trying to apply the lean manufacturing principle to my own business has been a fascinating journey. It has allowed us to really focus on the role of technology in our processes and how we deliver our events more seamlessly. At D&G, we're not making cars, but our business also has a series of processes designed to get us to the end product. So it matters to our clients how efficient those processes are. Put simply, Toyota's success and innovation is down to its focus on *kaizen*. It cares deeply about improving its processes as well as its products.

I could bore you (more) senseless with lots of other examples of businesses embracing *kaizen*. There are a considerable number of companies that do. I wanted to finish this chapter, though, with what this means for me and our business. It's the overall subject of this book, after all. Call it *kaizen*, marginal gains or – as Straussy refers to them – the one-per-centers; they all add up to the same thing. Building a culture in which everyone knows that everything can be improved. It is everyone's responsibility to make those tiny improvements at three levels; at the level of the individual, of the team and the company.

People are the greatest asset at our company, and they are what drive our business every day. They matter more than any physical asset or client or partner we have, and there are three things that I've come to realise about people over the years. The first is that almost everyone I've ever worked with is capable of much more than they think. They are also significantly more talented than they realise. They just need to feel valued and be given opportunities to shine. The second is that no one comes into the office to do a poor day's work or be deliberately miserable. Most people take immense pride in their work and what they do. Finally, you can tell a company by the people they keep. Marginal gains make a considerable difference to all three of these areas. By asking people to make small changes to the way they work, they improve very quickly. By giving people small areas of responsibility through which to grow, they develop their skills, and their confidence grows. Finally, by making incremental changes to your culture and your environment at work, you can significantly increase the number of people who want to stay with you. That's important for morale and your bottom line. The two are inextricably linked.

In my experience, the smaller and more frequent the gesture, the more significant the difference it makes to the team. I ask myself every day how I can help my team improve and make my company happier through tiny gestures and improvements. I make it my business to write a detailed and personalised Christmas card to all of our staff and suppliers. In it, I write about how they specifically have helped us that year and what they have done personally to make a difference. I know from people who work with us that it makes a huge difference that I take the time to do that. Perhaps not as much as the chocolate heart on every desk on Valentine's Day, but chocolate is always going to be more interesting than what I write! In those ways, I've followed *kaizen* to the letter over the years. It has made me a better leader. A few more tiny improvements over the next few years might mean that I become a half-decent boss! The concept of *kaizen* also makes demands of the individual. What are they doing to make the tiny changes to their lives and themselves that will propel them forward? Physically, mentally and in terms of their skills?

When it comes to teams, small incremental changes matter hugely. A team's job in any week is to make a better, faster decision than they did the week before. That might involve a small change to a briefing form or a decision to stand up rather than sit down in meetings to create more energy in the room. It could even be imagining that their biggest client has just fired them and working out what to do about that. It doesn't matter what the improvement is, provided it is tiny and often. As an aside, it's incredible how much more proactive people are when faced with real challenges. I was once in a meeting with someone who described the particular set of problems we were facing as 'a beautiful constraint'. His point was that tough situations require lateral thought and creative ingenuity. I liked the concept then, and I still do today. The most important thing a team can do to embrace *kaizen* is to understand that continuous improvement is the only way to guarantee long-term success.

For leaders faced with the challenge of creating a culture of continuous improvement for their businesses, there is one key issue. Find people who have what I referred to in an earlier chapter as a growth mindset. What does that mean? Well, it means finding people who see failure as an opportunity to improve. It means giving people a chance because they believe that they can learn to do anything they want. It is about having a company full of people who believe that effort and attitude determine their ability. Also, ones who believe that feedback is constructive and who feel inspired by the success of others. With this group of people and a culture built around *kaizen*, history and my own experience tell me that small, incremental improvements to people, teams and culture can yield extraordinary results.

Amazingly, the Japanese aren't a force in world cricket.

Chapter Six

ADAM

AT FIRST glance, this book is about my progression from being a journeyman professional cricketer to becoming an entrepreneur.

It is indeed about that progression, and my life in cricket taught me a vast amount about the role of leadership and what good leadership is. But, I also want this book to focus on what characteristics sport and business share and why that matters. Sport offers the individual a considerable amount. I've long argued that for young people, sport can provide a way of life and a way of thinking and behaving from a young age that will serve them well forever. Whether it's in the field of music, art, sport or drama, committing yourself to excellence in anything bears terrific fruit. You learn very quickly about success, failure, teamwork, discipline and effort, and they are all things that stay with you for life. I should know because I've had plenty of shockers along the way!

Chief among them was a harsh lesson I learned about friends in business. One of D&G's most treasured employees was Michelle Wallis. Michelle is no longer with us sadly, but I think about her every day, not least because her smiling face greets all of us at the top of the stairs each morning. It's a little framed reminder of what she meant to all of us. Some years ago, I wanted to support Michelle and her family and offered to help her husband with a new business venture. I bought him a grab lorry that cost me £30,000. I knew nothing about what these lorries did or how best to make money from them, but I trusted that he did. However, his business (and conduct) quickly became tricky and unsustainable and difficult conversations ensued. It wasn't easy, and I'll never forget how hard the conversation was with Michelle. Having to tell her that I couldn't support her husband anymore was horrible. The family are still great friends of ours. Michelle's daughter, Morgan, is a great pal of my daughter Sophie and always comes on holiday with us. Despite that, I'd never mix business with friendship like that again. It cost me £20,000 and also reminded me of the importance of the adage, 'You do best what you know best.'

Returning for a minute to the role sport can play in people's lives. If my business didn't exist today, I'd probably think about ways in which I could get more young people into sport. As a way of learning all of these incredibly valuable life lessons, there is no career equal. The world would be a happier place, and the streets would be safer if more young people found their voice through sport. I love it when I see kids playing it, enjoying it and learning from it.

I was fortunate because my testimonial year gave me the idea, the knowledge and the impetus to set up the D&G group. Initially, the D&G stood for my and my brother's names, David and Glen, as I've mentioned already. One day, one of my closest pals and someone who was working with us on a consultancy basis at the time, Simon Pavitt, said that he thought those letters were about much more. So they became the words that today stand at the very centre of what we do, namely Delivering and Giving. They represent everything we care about, and they are an excellent guide for anyone coming into our business because they describe our purpose. This subject will feature heavily in the next chapter. In a nutshell, our company supports some of the UK's leading brands in hosting their charity events. However, we've become much more than that now. We think of ourselves as a seamless integration between corporate and charity fund-raising. Although our group has now grown with related businesses in events, silent auctions, consultancy and hospitality, our purpose is essentially the same. We give something back.

As I say, I was lucky, and it's certainly true that, from an early age, some young sportsmen and women are thinking about their lives outside of sport. They should be doing that because sport is a short-lived career with plenty of risks attached. Again, one of the areas I'd be focusing on at any club today is the extent to which I would be helping my young professionals plan for the future. I'll be honest and say that I haven't seen many examples across sport where this is taken as seriously as it should be. For the young cricketer though, they have a massive opportunity because, for six months of the year, they can explore other countries, companies and opportunities. Across a 15-year career, a young cricketer today could visit seven or eight countries and gain internships across seven or eight different companies. By the time they got to the age of 35, that would be an impressive CV and certainly one that I'd sit up and notice. All it takes is for those young people to have a plan. 'A man without a plan is no plan at all,' as I read once.

The list of people who have made the transition from sport to business is full of individuals much smarter, more prosperous and more famous than me. I wonder how many people today walk into a David Lloyd club knowing that their founder was one of the most successful British tennis players in the 70s and 80s. As a coach, he was also partly responsible for Tim Henman's rise to the top of the game.

Some sportsmen start businesses while they are still playing as a way of investing some of their earnings, and that was undoubtedly true for footballer Robbie Fowler. After a glittering career with Liverpool, Robbie became a big player in the UK property market. I have it on good authority that many of the Liverpool fans used to sing 'We all live in a Robbie Fowler house' to the tune of 'Yellow Submarine'. Love that. By 2005, Robbie was in the *Sunday Times* Rich List with an estimated wealth of £28 million.

Our revenue is a drop in the ocean compared to that. I knew by my mid-twenties that I enjoyed the entrepreneurial 'thrill of the chase'. A cricket coaching business was quickly followed by a venture into the travel industry. I took a group of clients to the Ashes Down Under. We got hammered, and Warney took his 700th test wicket (which happened to be that of Straussy), but we had a great time. My first real profitable business, I guess. There was significant risk in having to secure the flights and hotels up front, but I backed myself to sell them. I'm glad I did. By the end of the trip, I'd made a very tidy profit. I knew then that I could make money from the skills I had.

More recently, you can see further evidence of the link between sport and business. Indra Nooyi, the chairman of PepsiCo, played cricket at college in India. Mark Zuckerberg was captain of his high school fencing team, and Meg Whitman, the former CEO of Hewlett Packard, was a competitive swimmer. If you look over the pond as well, you see fascinating evidence of the link between female leadership and competitive sports. A 2015 study conducted by espnW and EY looked at 400 female C-suite individuals (funny phrase but it means leaders apparently). The study found a massive link between sporting and business success. More than half of the female leaders surveyed played sport at university level, compared to 39% of women at other management levels. The same study also found that 80% of female 'Fortune 500' leaders played competitive sport at one time in their lives. Women's sport, of course, is leading the way in bringing equality front and centre stage. Across almost every major female team sport now, audiences are growing, and the sponsorship deals are getting bigger. It's still not enough, and there's a long way to go, but I'm enjoying watching women lead from the front in sport and business. I think women make better leaders than men, given what I've experienced over the last decade. Women have more empathy than men; they are better team players, and they are natural communicators. I also think they have a greater instinct for how you develop culture, a subject to which I'll come back.

It's clear then that there's lots of evidence to support the basic thesis of this book. Sport and business are inextricably linked and provide a platform for mutual success. Over the last few years, I've given much thought as to why, and I've landed on five essential runways. In other words, five areas where sport allows you to develop skills that help you take off in business. Forgive the word play. I failed my A-level English, remember.

The first critical skill that you develop as an elite sportsman is to accept that failure and mistakes are part of the process. This skill is never more true than in the world of cricket. Being a batsman is arguably one of the hardest things to do in professional sport. One lapse in concentration, one tiny error of judgement, one mistake by the umpire and your day is over. Almost every batsman in the world will fail more than they succeed. The scar tissue associated with batting can often be challenging to handle, and I know that from personal experience. You have to see the bigger picture and accept that you will get out more than you will reach the magical three figures. The single most important thing to realise though is that every dismissal is an opportunity to learn something about yourself, your batting and the bowlers you're facing. It's also an opportunity to build the most important muscle in your body, resilience.

Straussy was a master at this. If you saw him at the end of a day's play, you'd have no idea whether he had got out first ball or hit a big double hundred, such was his demeanour. Ben Hutton was precisely the opposite. A big personal score would mean you couldn't get him out of the bar despite his reputation for being the tightest man at Lord's. My nickname for him was 'Crime' because it doesn't pay. A low score would mean Ben became Lord Lucan and a mute Lord Lucan at that.

Grit and determination are the difference between the good and the great in my opinion, and it's only by failing that you can accept it as part of the process of improving.

Having this experience has given me so much in my career. It's allowed me to remain calm in the face of business adversity, and it's allowed me to help others to put things into perspective. We've lost clients, pitches and excellent people over the years of running D&G because of mistakes that we've made but we've always come back stronger. 'That which doesn't break you makes you stronger,' as the saying goes. I believe that from the bottom of my heart.

My second 'learning runway' has been all about teams. Elite team sport is not about the individual, and when it is, those teams become toxic environments. I've been in dressing rooms just like that. A team sport is about a group of very talented individuals coming together to win – all with different skills and different goals. My business today is precisely the same. We are fortunate to have some fantastic people who work hard, challenge everything and have a real desire to win. My professional cricket career taught me that you need different people with different skills in various roles. Spotting where to put people so that you give them the best chance to succeed is critical. Without that, you can never build a winning team or a successful business.

I've sat in many a dressing room after a substantial loss with that horrid sinking feeling that you can only get after a defeat. It teaches you two things very quickly – how to be humble and how to be accountable. Humility is an excellent trait in business as it is in life. It wins you friends; it buys you time to succeed, and it makes for a happier environment all round. You soon learn in sport that humility is essential because the next match can find you out very quickly. The same is true in business. As I say to my teams as often as I can, you are only ever three phone calls away from disaster in business. Or a pandemic. Our company would be on code red if our three biggest clients fired us simultaneously. That kind of humility keeps people honest and grounded, two traits I admire in people.

The other thing sport teaches you quickly is that you have to be accountable for your actions. There are no hiding places on the pitch or the scorecard. It's there for all to see. If you've had a stinker, no one needs to tell you about it, but it is vital that you acknowledge it; for your sake and everyone else's. It makes for a more honest environment. In my experience, the best people know that they are responsible and accountable for their actions. In my business career, I've tried to make this a constant theme. Responsibility without accountability is about as useful as the old chocolate fireguard.

Eoin Morgan is a brilliant cricketer and captain. I played with him, Billy Godleman and Steve Finn in the same team. All youngsters coming up through the ranks together. Since then, I've admired from a distance Eoin's stewardship of the England team. I do believe that his handling of the Alex Hales drugs situation before the recent World Cup was one of the main reasons that England were victorious. I knew that they were destined to lift the trophy when the whole squad and staff turned up to run the Ruth Strauss Foundation Family Mile, finishing in front of Buckingham Palace, two days before their first game. A class act from a group of exceptional people which demonstrated huge unity.

What goes around does come around, as the saying goes. As well as being very decisive, Eoin is also a man who stays very calm under pressure. That ability alone will serve him well when he eventually hangs up his boots. The ability to remain calm under pressure is something that all great sportsmen and women have to learn. The wicketkeeper reminding you of your last four low scores as you're facing the first ball (me basically!) The final over of a game needing 15 to win, or just the ball which is travelling towards you at speed and knowing that if you drop it, you've let your entire team down. This ability to be composed is critical in business. If you panic as a leader, so will everyone else. If you show that you're worried, everyone will assume that the worst has happened. Stay calm, be composed, and you will have much more natural authority.

Quite often, that authority leads to a confidence and assuredness that is truly exceptional. Never was this more true than with Glenn McGrath. I had the pleasure of playing with Glenn for one season at Middlesex and the bloke was a legend. When bowling in the nets, he'd often call the delivery he was about to make and nail it every time. He was a smart cookie, too, with a hugely competitive streak. So much so that he turned my quirky superstitions to his advantage when I played against him while he was at Worcester dropping leaves, sweet wrappers and anything else in his pocket around the wicket as he knew that anything in my eyeline would throw me into a mental meltdown.

Finally, before we move on to ADAM, the last interplay between sport and business that I've come to recognise as very important is the ability not to look back. Teams win and lose, but the best ones always focus on the next game and the next opportunity. A few years ago, Mark Zuckerberg and his team released their Snapchat competitor, 'Slingshot' – it was an abject failure. However, they moved on quickly, and today they have Instagram, which has proven to be real competition to Snapchat. Top-class performers don't dwell on the past, whether it's negative or positive. They worry about what's in front of them, the next day, week and year. That's true for me today but only because I learned the hard way through sport.

I mentioned ADAM just now. Not because it's a name I like (although I don't dislike it), nor because one of my business partners is called Adam. It's because, since becoming an entrepreneur, it's the process that I've realised separates great businesses from not so great ones. We are lucky enough to have worked with some fantastic clients over the years, and I have worked with some incredible people and companies. Abellio, Argos, ASOS, Bidfood, Holland & Barrett, and Iceland Foods among them. Beyond that, there was Rolls-Royce and Homebase together with some fantastic charities including Macmillan, Nordoff Robbins and the British Heart Foundation. Our clients have always been fair and honest with us. Demanding, of course, but always willing to work as partners even when things go wrong. I'll never forget our first major Bidfood event for that reason.

When the CEO, Andrew Selley, turned up at the golf day very early to check all was well, he discovered that we had branded everything with the name Bidvest. It's possibly the worst mistake we could have made. I didn't know this until his speech at the gala dinner that night when he referenced the mistake. My team had sorted it quickly in the morning as soon as they realised but I was still mortified. I remember going to see our primary client contact, Tim Adams, straight away after the main course to take the mistake on the chin and tell him that he should probably fire us. He admired my honesty I think, because he gave us a second chance the following year. They are still a valued client of ours today. It's a good lesson in fronting your mistakes early and, as the boss, taking responsibility for them.

To every single one of our clients and partners, I can't thank you enough for this kind, unwavering support over so many years. Working with you has taught me so much. I do hope the pages of this book do justice to that. We're not perfect at D&G by any stretch, but we will always go the extra mile for you, and we never take your support or your business for granted. Alongside the good ones, we've also met some pretty duff businesses along the way, and the difference is incredible. Good companies have a vision, great people, real energy, they communicate well, and they seek partners from whom they can learn. I've come to realise over the years that great businesses also have a friend called ADAM too. Let me explain.

In almost every walk of life, including sport, in your home and your business, four parts make up the sum of anything you might do. You analyse a situation, you decide what to do, you act on that decision, and then you measure the impact of it. Analyse, Decide, Act, Measure. ADAM. The ADAM loop as I call it because here's the thing. The key difference I've noticed between the good and not so good in business is the speed and frequency with which companies move around that loop. Good companies make it their business to complete as many ADAM loops as possible across their critical strategic priorities. Weak companies get stuck by analysing everything and doing nothing. Others don't do enough analysis, and in lots of cases, companies don't bother to measure anything. 'That which doesn't get measured never gets done,' as they say.

The point is that for weak companies, there is either no attempt to embrace an ADAM loop or they don't get around the loop as often as they should in any given year. It's why in our business today, we spend as much time analysing as we do measuring. It's also why we are happy to launch new divisions and test new markets because the ADAM loop allows us to make informed decisions and act on them. I despair of organisations (and sometimes my own) in which decisions aren't made fast enough or acted upon quickly enough. For me, the answer always lies with the ADAM loop. Where are we on the loop? How quickly can we move around it? Lots of the decisions I used to make were from my gut. I've learned to my cost that this doesn't always work. I suspect it's why I came up with the ADAM loop in the first place.

One man's attempt to justify a different way of working and hide his inefficiencies! One of the critical aspects of using the ADAM loop is to assess how good you are at each part. Do we have the intellectual firepower in our business to analyse well? Do we have enough people with excellent decision-making skills? Are our systems geared up to implement the decisions we make? Finally, and perhaps most importantly, do we know what we are measuring and why? All four of these questions are crucial to growing and maintaining a successful business.

The interesting thing about the ADAM loop is that I wish I'd thought of it while I was still playing professional cricket. It would have helped me, and it might even have helped the club for whom I played. How much real analysis happened, I'm not sure. Still, even today, I see clubs making decisions that seem to bear no relation to any measurement criteria. Batsmen with poor averages being played week in, week out because of their career average. This is a nonsense, in my opinion. Look forward, not back. Test and learn. Try something different and then measure it. Worse still, I meet businesses which are almost Jurassic in their ability to make decisions quickly. They seem to be afraid of making decisions for fear of making the wrong ones. That's not my style, and it's not an environment in which I'd ever work. Embracing the ADAM loop gives companies tremendous momentum, energy and something on which to focus. Maybe I should trademark it and join the speaker circuit: just me, ADAM and a flipchart. There's a thought for my retirement.

Chapter Seven

What's the Point?

'THE TWO most important days in your life are the day that you are born, and the day you find out why.'

Mark Twain.

'Most men lead lives of quiet desperation and go to their graves with their song still in them.'

Henry David Thoreau.

If I had two quotes to pick that have made the most significant impact on the way I've built my business and lived my life, these two would be right up there. Within these quotes, you'll find the importance of living each day. You'll also find the importance of doing what you're best at but most importantly, doing all you can to discover the real reason you get up every day. It's one of life's significant challenges, but finding your real purpose does give you a reason to live. I now know how much purpose matters for people and businesses. However, finding your purpose is very hard, which is why I guess most men and women go to their graves with their song still in them.

Looking back on it, I don't think that cricket was ever my real purpose in life. Perhaps a shocking thing for me to admit now. Like many young people, I was carried along by my dad's enthusiasm for the game, my mum's drive to help me and an ability to hit the ball. Yes, I was good enough at cricket (and a few other sports as well), and I found myself playing at a high level, but I'm not sure that I ever loved it. I loved everything around it: the lads, the banter, the beers, the trips, but the game itself? I'm not sure. Perhaps that's why I became so interested in the whole concept of purpose. 'What am I going to do next?' was a question that used to occupy me a great deal but which I didn't discuss with many people.

Cricket and indeed professional sport when I played was an environment which didn't embrace vulnerability or weakness. From the way the teams were given less than flattering names in the early morning football warm-ups to the mental abuse (yes, I did use that word) that you received from some of your team-mates and captains. It wasn't right.

Since retiring, I've thought a great deal about this and it's a tricky one. On the one hand, I do know that I played in a different era to the one we're in now and for that reason, I deliberately haven't named names. At this point, I've got Ed Smith's advice at the beginning of this book ringing in my ears. On the other hand, I've come to realise that if you're not part of the solution, you're part of the problem and in that sense, I got it wrong. I should have called it out more and I should have tried to put the issues I was most worried about at the top of the dressing room agenda. Lots of people from my era suffered in different ways.

Given the pressure I felt during my career, I sometimes look back and wonder how I ever managed to have such a long one and survive almost intact. I guess Middlesex must have been thin on the ground for wicketkeepers who could hold a bat! Many of these earlier experiences stayed with me, and I promised myself that whatever I did after cricket would make me happier and more mentally robust.

I think part of my story and perhaps part of my motivation in business was that I wasted a great deal of natural talent as a young man. I signed for Middlesex when I was just 15. I was a prolific batsman in the England age groups, and the numbers don't lie on that front. IIn my final tour for England under 19's in Pakistan, I was the stand out batsman on that trip with Chris Read taking the gloves. 108 not out in the first innings of the second test match at the Sheikhupura Stadium followed by 87 in the second innings; run out as well so pretty close to back to back hundreds which would have been great. We had a great bunch of lads, with players like Flintoff, Harmison and Tudor. It was then that I got involved in the drinking groups and never really recovered from that. My Zimbabwe tour probably demonstrated that better than most times. The irrepressible David Lloyd (Bumble as he's better known) was our coach and gave me as bad an end of tour report as ever I had at school. Hardly surprising given that I nearly missed the flight home due to a banging hangover and also ended up behind a sightscreen throwing my guts up on the morning of one game after my birthday night out. Not the behaviour of a model athlete or a likely future England star.

Those tours were memorable for all kinds of reasons but particularly because of the people with whom I was lucky enough to play. Ben Hollioake was one of those people. A great cricketer and an even better bloke who sadly left us far too soon. I was playing for Fremantle in Perth when the devastating news came through that Ben had lost his life in a car crash. It was the same horrible sinking feeling I had when I heard that Umer Rashid, the Middlesex and Sussex cricketer, had died in a swimming accident. These are moments that you never forget. The circle of life is sometimes a reminder that shocking things happen to lovely people. This was never more true than when my great mate Hitch died aged 42. It was a sudden and pretty brutal death from liver failure brought on by a virus and not something that I'll ever really come to terms with. The shock, sleepless nights and subsequent anxiety I felt around his death have subsided but the pain never really goes away when you lose someone you love. You just learn to live with it. Finding ways of marking how important these people were really matters to me. In Hitch's case, we now play an annual memorial game against Oli Slipper's club, Weybridge. Oli is a good friend and successful entrepreneur from whom I've learned lots about business and life. Through that annual event, we've now set up a fund to sponsor a young cricketer keen to get experience abroad who might not otherwise be able to afford it. It's these little touches that add real meaning to some of life's hard-to-understand moments.

I enjoyed life away from the cricket too much and never really took it seriously enough. Looking back now, I hate to think of the number of games where I turned up drunk. In those days too, you'd go out on the Saturday before a Sunday League game and roll in at 2am at the earliest. Up the next day, full English and straight to the ground. Hardly a beacon of professionalism shining brightly around me! Hardly a beacon of professionalism shining brightly around me! You wouldn't get away with it these days although I do worry that the game has become too sanitised. Speak to any of the players of my era, and they will tell you that the best way to get over a miserable day's cricket was to talk it out over a pint. Some of the most insightful things I ever picked up were from the older players over a beer. I just wonder how many young players today have that outlet and can wind down properly after a day's play. It's a vital part of maintaining your well-being. A reminder that it's only a game and you get paid to play what we used to call 'games' at school. I touched on this earlier in the book, and I hope all counties are taking this issue seriously. We've moved from the era of sports psychology to the age of mental well-being. Players need support, and they need an environment in which they feel able to talk about their issues, challenges and anxieties. If you're a CEO of any sports team reading this, please take note. It should be your number one priority with every single one of your players.

Eventually, I knew my time as a county cricketer was coming to an end, and so I decided to be as proactive as I could. I went to see Vinny Codrington, the then Middlesex CEO, and pitched him an idea for my final contract. I offered to take a pay cut providing I could have a three-year deal with a testimonial year at the end. I also offered to work with the club and their sponsors over the winters on a commission-only basis. It turned out to be the best deal I ever did and a complete game-changer for me because it allowed me to get to know the club's sponsors and build great relationships with them. It introduced me to the real world of business. I knew immediately that I had found something that I might love, and so it turned out to be. In those early days, the idea behind D&G was born.

I had one other light bulb moment in these formative years, and that was my first visit to my local Shooting Star Children's Hospice in 2007. This charity became a defining moment in my journey, and my first visit is one I'll never forget. In case you're not familiar with it, Shooting Star is a charity dedicated to caring for babies, children and young people with life-limiting conditions. It's an extraordinary charity full of exceptional people who don't need to read either of the quotes at the beginning of this chapter. They have purpose coursing through their veins, and they make an incredible difference to other people's lives. The stories I heard and the people I met that day certainly changed my life. My testimonial meant that I could donate £25,000 to them that year and I'm proud to say that we've raised hundreds of thousands of pounds since then. I'm hugely proud to be associated with them, as is our business.

My testimonial year was the final piece of the purpose jigsaw if you like. It was a huge success and even as a player without international honours, I broke the benefit year record at Middlesex. It convinced me that I could build relationships, raise money, and it also opened my eyes to a gap in the corporate world. Lots of businesses quite rightly cared about corporate social responsibility. Lots of them wanted to do more to help charities by organising golf days and dinners. Yet, within each organisation, no one was driving this ambition. It was often a role given to someone to look after in their spare time. So opportunities were being lost, and the chance to raise money for incredibly worthy causes squandered.

It didn't take me long to see the gap in the market, and D&G was born. Nine years later, we've raised over £20m a year for those causes, and we have a business turning over £8m. How has that happened? Great people, yes. A considerable amount of hard work, yes. Perhaps the biggest reason though is that my brother and I had given ourselves a real purpose. In turn, we'd started a business whose purpose got us out of bed in the mornings. Given we started the company from mum and dad's spare bedroom in Sunbury, we didn't have a long commute in the early days!

So, the subject of purpose and its role in all of our lives is very close to my heart. I'll tell you what I've learned about it over the years in the hope that it gives the three people who might read this book some food for thought. I mentioned in the first chapter that Simon Sinek's book *Start with Why* was a significant influence in my business thinking. In it, he develops his idea of the 'Golden Circle'. He's interested in why some companies sell more even despite the fact that their competition is as good. He's also interested in why some leaders are more influential than others. Two subjects that I became hugely interested in as I started my business.

Sinek is an ex-adman (don't hold that against him). His book is a study of the success of some of the world's leading and influential leaders and how they and their organisations think, act and communicate. His model is that of the Golden Circle, and he argues this. Most companies

Every day I get to work I see this amazing lady's smiling face. Her photo welcomes us into the D&G office. She was the most selfless, giving, and hard-working person I've known. She will be forever missed but certainly not forgotten. The Michelle Wallis Award at work is the one to be won.

Receiving my commemorative Middlesex County cap for 16 years of service to this great club from my cricketing hero Mike Gatting. I couldn't say no when big Gus Fraser and Straussy asked for a photo with me!

At the Middlesex 150th anniversary game versus MCC with the legends, Mum and Dad, who sacrificed so much for me to live out my dreams and put up with all my shit! I'm so gutted my three youngest daughters Sophie, Annabelle and Lottie couldn't see me play more for the club we all love.

Glen and I at the ASOS golf day with the founder Nick Robertson and CEO Nick Beighton. I learnt so much from them as they are standout people who are a perfect example of what a great partnership can do. For me that applies to working every day with my brother who I trust with my life.

With the England Under-15s at Newlands, my second-favourite ground after Lord's. Great memories with Messrs Sales, Tudor, Batty and Flintoff, with whom I shared a match-winning partnership to beat South Africa.

With Straussy and his eldest boy Sam and Sophie in Melbourne at the 2006/07 Ashes. Like her mum, Sophie looks like she is enjoying the Crown Lager more than Sam. Straussy certainly needed a few after a 5-0 thrashing!

Running the London Marathon for the third time in aid of Shooting Star Chase Children's Hospice for whom I'm proud to be an ambassador. I love taking on challenges such as The Grim and Tough Mudder to raise much-needed funds for great causes. We could all do more!

Dad's 80th birthday at ours with Glen and his amazing family; wife Leann and my nephews Freddie and Bobby and niece Georgie. To celebrate with Mum and Dad and tell them how much we love them in front of all their friends was very emotional but a highlight.

At my 40th with all five of my amazing daughters – Leah, Emily, Sophie, Annabelle and Lottie – alongside my rock, Jules. I'm so blessed to have such a supportive and loving family and friends.

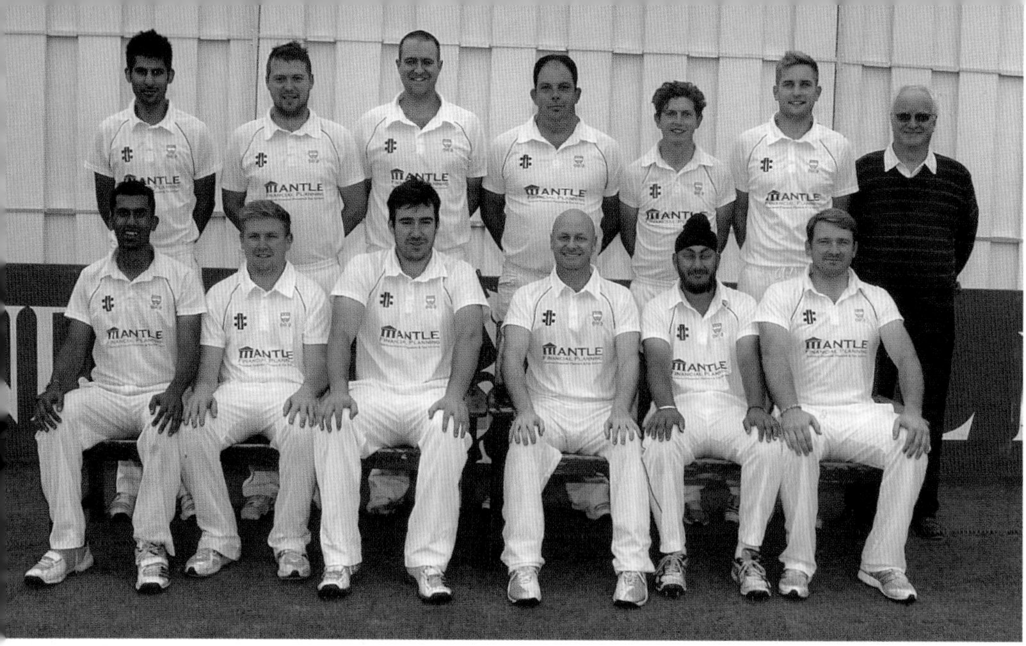

This photo was taken shortly before my most gutting moment on the cricket field well after I retired. Losing the national final with my beloved club Sunbury was gut-wrenching as I so wanted to win this with my mates, Maundo, Grange, Junior, Ratty, Smudge, Londers, etc., for the great man Frank Sharman who did so much for me and all these guys. He was a true gentleman who taught us all the right values.

In Antigua at the Stanford T20 with Scotty, Morgy, Richo, Carts, Mala and Finny. I knew that Alan Stanford was a wrong 'un the moment I met him – if he was made of chocolate, he'd eat himself! Eoin Morgan on the other hand showed his class even back then. He was always captain material in my mind.

With our Argos clients, Chris Corbin and CEO John Walden. One of the funniest lines came from England captain and legend Graham Gooch (pictured), 'Who would have thought all these years ago, Nashy, I'd be bloody driving you around!' I nicknamed him Ivor the driver, priceless!

*With Harry Potter and the lads in the changing room after winning the T20 in 2008. I personally did f**k all – Scotty had deservedly taken the gloves by then but I'm always up for a celebration when Middlesex win something. On this occasion with my great pals, Scotty, Shah, Murts, Finny, Shaggy and Muz.*

In Perth with Jules many years ago, where I played for Fremantle. As I said I'm shit at everything, but I've always managed to find the best people to surround myself with, as said by the late, great Don McCarthy. This couldn't be truer than in relation to my amazing wife Jules. I decided to acknowledge all she's brought to my life by including this photo I know she's going to hate!

have no idea why customers choose their products. Most successful companies focus on three key questions to drive success. WHAT, HOW, WHY. All very obvious up to this point. What he then discovers though lies at the heart of why having a purpose matters. Most companies start with the WHAT; in other words, the products or services a company sells. They then focus on the HOW; why their products/services are better or stand out from the competition. Lastly, the company concentrates on the WHY, meaning what the company believes in and why it exists. Inspired and influential companies, Sinek argues, start with the WHY.

Sinek demonstrates his Golden Circle by using Apple as an example. Apple starts with the WHY, the centre of the Golden Circle. So, instead of communicating what they do and how they do it, they communicate their vision to their potential buyers. As a company, they think differently so that they can challenge the status quo. They then move on to the HOW by telling their potential buyers that their eye-catching designs are easy to use. Finally, they get to their WHAT: they make computers. Ultimately, Sinek argues that customers do not buy products because of what companies do but because of why they do it. My own experience tells me this too.

Iceland sells over £1 billion of frozen food products a year, but they have a very clear WHY. They are committed to 'doing the right thing' in four key areas. Their supply chain, their people, their customers and environmentally. Most recently, under the new leadership of Richard Walker, they became the first major retailer in the world to commit to eliminating plastic packaging from its own-label products by 2023. Iceland is a company with real purpose.

So, what's my purpose, and what's our company's purpose? Before I come to that, one more observation about what purpose means for the individual and business. Many books exist on this topic, and there are no end of self-help videos online. The golden bullet is about finding something that you're good at, something you love and something that ultimately pays the bills. That's the popular theory, and it's right, of course. There's one more element that only the Japanese (a popular theme in this book!) have nailed.

The fourth and arguably most crucial pillar of purpose is to do something that the world needs. There has been no moment in recent human history where this is more the case. Our planet is in meltdown (literally and metaphorically) and the advent of artificial intelligence is challenging our understanding of what work is and what it is to be human.

Creativity, collaboration and critical thinking are all things that will separate the good from the great in the 21st century, and those things will differentiate us from machines. But what will matter most is our individual and collective responsibility to make a difference to other people and the planet. And this is where the Japanese come in. They are so smart that they even have a word for the four critical pillars of purpose, *ikigai*. The quest to find something you love, something you're good at, something that makes money and something the world needs.

I'm very proud that my brother and I and hopefully many of our colleagues have found our *ikigai*. Simon Sinek would be proud of us. I think this is because, from day one, we started with our WHY. To give something back. We realised very quickly that our purpose needed to extend to four key groups of stakeholders. They were our colleagues, our partners, our clients and the charities we worked with. From day one, we've tried as hard as we can to crack all four. We've done so by working hard, keeping our purpose in sight at all times and finding brilliant partners and clients. We've all got 20 million reasons to get us up in the morning. It's the next £20 million that we're going to raise that excites me most. One of the final observations I'd make about our purpose is this. It has been relatively easy to think about other areas of business that might interest us and be consistent about what motivates us. Our new recruitment business, for example, offers companies the opportunity to donate part of our fee to a charity of their choice once we place a candidate. That's another version of giving back that excites us, and I'm looking forward to building a group full of these kinds of companies in the future.

Giving something back is an ever-present part of our company's ethos and it's important to me that we live this every day. It's why we developed 'D&G Smiles', a concept that allows us to put time and money towards making people smile who otherwise might not have much to smile about and in doing so, make a difference to their lives. This part of our company has allowed us to sponsor a young Sri Lankan girl to help with her education. Closer to home, we also gave a young man who was brutally stabbed for nothing but his phone the opportunity to see his favourite football team, Aston Villa, in the 2020 Carabao Cup Final. These opportunities to make a difference really are the things that keep me going.

One of the real reasons that I like the concept of purpose is that it eliminates a great deal of bullshit from corporate life (the major theme of another chapter in this book). 'Why do you exist?' is a simple question which requires a simple answer. Getting to that answer is hard though, and I'd argue that lots of companies that exist today either can't answer that question or even if they can, it's bullshit. Ours isn't. It's obvious, and everyone understands it in a heartbeat. If you're reading this and you want to know the only four questions that you should be asking of your business, here they are;

What do you do?

Why do you do it?

How do you do it?

What do you focus on?

As a dusty ex-professional cricketer, I find it weird to be offering up nuggets of business advice. Still, I guess that's what this book is trying to do. This chapter's theme, purpose, is one very close to my heart and one which I've been a student of for some years, so you'll forgive the advice, I hope. Going from a life in professional cricket with a minimal purpose to a career in business full of reasons to get out of bed has been a fantastic journey. It's happened because I was willing to open my eyes to possibilities, and I was ready to go after them proactively. In the end, without action, there can be no purpose. No amount of sitting around hoping that the answer will come to you will work. You have to go and make it happen yourself.

Chapter Eight

'Culture Eats Strategy for Breakfast'

IF YOU'VE read this far, well done! If you've decided to start at this chapter, good luck. Either way, a quick summary of what we've covered to date might help. Kevin Pietersen, Langer's advice and Japan. Bacon butties, Jürgen Klopp, why I can't explain my nickname Knocker in a book like this, Socrates and psychopaths. So, if you have just joined us, look what you've missed! To be serious for a minute, though. I've now explained a bit about me, what I've learned about leadership and why I believe that the way to make the most significant difference is by focusing on small improvements consistently. Finally, I hope I've given you some insights into why purpose matters to me and why I'm so excited about the journey to come for my business. You should also know by now that I quite like Japan!

When I decided to write this book, it's fair to say that I had a mixed reaction. Some didn't realise that I could write, some thought I had nothing to say for myself and others wondered how I'd get away with writing a sentence without the word 'dog' in it. That's how I refer to most people you see, as a term of endearment or because I've forgotten their name! It's incredible how quickly people get used to it. The more generous-spirited of my friends thought it was a good idea, although a few of them were worried that I would spill the beans on our antics over the years. I'd never do that to a pal, particularly not to help sell a book. However, grab me at Lord's over a pint, and I'll sing like a canary! 'But who the f*** is going to read your drivel?' asked one kindly soul. That generous soul being Jules, worryingly.

Well, it did get me thinking. Who will read it, and does it matter? I concluded that it didn't matter who read it because just the process of me putting a lifetime of learning on the page was going to be quite a journey for me. Writing my thoughts down would help me frame them properly and would probably allow me to realise how much I have learned over the years. I hope my mates read it and use it as an opportunity to take the mickey forever. More than that, I hope some young cricketers read it because, at least in some of the pages, I can offer some timely words of advice. I also hope some of my clients read it so that they can see a different side of me. The jovial, happy-go-lucky Nashy has been learning on the job for ten years and is maybe starting to see the bigger picture.

My biggest hope is that our team at D&G read it because it's a decade of business wrapped up in probably too many words. To everyone who works or has ever worked with us, as we tell you all of the time, you are our second family. I hope we demonstrate that every day; without our fantastic team helping us to grow the business, we don't have much, to be honest. We rely on you, and we couldn't be more grateful for the support you give us.

Finally, maybe even my family will read it if only to convince themselves that I can write! In the end, I hope for whoever reads it, this book does what it says on the tin. I hope it provides a few insights into what sport gave me and how it's helped me build my various entrepreneurial ventures. 'Doing what it says on the tin.' That sounds like a neat link into a chapter about culture.

No chapter about culture would be right unless it started with a massive nod to D&G's first chairman, Mike Tobin. Mike was a hugely influential person in our formative years and probably the most crucial decision we made back then. Mike is a technology entrepreneur, author and philanthropist so understood our business immediately. In 2014, he was awarded an OBE for services to the digital economy. He has been widely recognised as a 'Third Sector Business Charity Champion' for his fund-raising work with many charities including the Prince's Trust, Action for Children and the British Asian Trust.

In 2016, Mike ran 40 marathons in 40 days, raising over £100,000 for charity. He's an exceptional human being as well as being a world-class businessman. In his book *Forget Strategy. Get Results*, he talks about the importance of culture. His view is that while you can teach skills, you can't teach culture or mindset and so these are the two most important things to focus on as a leader. I've learned so much from being around him, talking to him and hearing his views across a range of business topics. He and I also share a very similar view of the world of education. You no longer need to teach children facts and knowledge but instead, teach them how to navigate the world. They need a deep understanding of how to engage, empathise and use creativity to build value. Mike remains one of my and D&G's most trusted advisors and, for many years, was the first call I'd make when I knew I had a problem to solve. His faith in me and our business over the years has been like magic dust.

I've known many people who don't need to read this chapter, and Mike Tobin is one of them. Sadly, I met lots of people in cricket who would benefit from reading this chapter. Why? Well, because it's all about culture and how, in the end, if you build the right one, anything's possible. I must say that I learned masses from seeing how not to do it, so I guess I owe a big thank you to the players and coaches who got it badly wrong. Having experienced both ends of the spectrum, I'm now reasonably well qualified to comment on what works and what doesn't, in sport and business. And even if I'm not, I'm going to anyway!

'The way we do things around here' is one way I've heard culture described. There are plenty of others. Usually, but not exclusively, culture consists of a set of shared values and a set of beliefs that impact every aspect of the working or sporting environment. Culture also cuts across day-to-day behaviours, and most importantly, the strength of any culture determines how difficult or easy it is to know how to behave in any given environment. The proximity of a changing room amplifies this issue. It makes building the right culture even more difficult in sport.

There are any number of areas that reflect the culture of a business. These include how companies recruit colleagues, and how they look after their visitors and guests (or supporters). It also consists of the physical space around you and how much responsibility is given to individuals. How long people stay in a business is an excellent marker of a business's culture, as is the way you negotiate contracts. The personality and style of your sales force says everything about you as does how quickly you respond and what method of communication you use. How staff interact with each other and the quality of your marketing materials are essential. The speed with which you make decisions and the number of layers in the management structure are also significant determiners of culture. So, the list is pretty long, and as a leader, you have to be mindful of all of them. Over the years, in sport and business, I've witnessed brilliant examples of top cultural environments.

Here, every colleague understands what they need to do and why. In those environments, there's little need for policies and procedures, and you see very consistent levels of behaviour. Seen from the other end of the cultural telescope, however, it's a very different picture. Poor culture sees almost no alignment with the values of the business or team. You see hugely inconsistent behaviour and a rocky path for new people coming in. Culture is tough to crack, and you have to focus on it relentlessly. I've learned this the hard way through starting my own business, but it's now one of my major priorities as a leader. It's probably my top priority.

I witnessed so many examples of poor culture through my years in cricket that I'm not sure where to start. Ian 'Gunner' Gould (our second XI coach) would regularly call me out very aggressively in front of the senior players. He did it deliberately to make me feel small and embarrassed. Those were the days of the school of hard knocks, but they were the beginning of my real anxieties. As much as I enjoy Gunner's company today, I can't forgive him for the damage he did to me and some of the cricketers around me. Even my mate Gus Fraser sometimes got to me. He refused me access to the dining room one day after years of service to the club because I wasn't playing for the first team. I was so livid that I thrust the £29.50 that I knew it cost the club to feed us into his pocket and stormed upstairs to eat. I refused to spend the £10 expenses we got as second-team players on a shit burger and chips. I was a professional cricketer and wanted to eat like one. The last words Gus heard from me as I headed up to the players' dining room were 'Fuck you Gus, I might be shit and in the 2s but we need to eat as well.' In those days, I was always charm personified.

I've been in a team that changed its selection policy to bring in someone new just before one of the biggest games of all of our lives. I've seen the captain who most people fear because of his arrogance and total focus on himself and the coach who seemed happy to tolerate second best.

My time in sport was very revealing. I developed a clear understanding of what does and does not drive high-performance culture in a sporting context.

If I were leading a team today, this would be my blueprint. Firstly, it is the coach's responsibility to create the culture they want. Either by asking the players to draw up their charter as Straussy did or to craft it themselves. I know from bitter experience that culture never just happens or emerges. If it does, it is usually toxic. The coach and leader have to, very clearly, define their values and behaviours, and these must match the goals that the team want to achieve. Perhaps most importantly, these teams must have captains who model these values and practices. Without that, nothing will work, and I can think of at least one instance recently in county cricket where the captain did anything but model the right behaviours. Not surprisingly, that team struggled against all expectation. A fish does rot from its head. In every instance, when asked to write down the words to describe themselves, every member of a team should write down words such as accountable, responsible and honest. The team should spend time focusing on the effort, not the result. The best sporting environments that I've seen are ones in which the players have ownership over the team's direction and they, first and foremost, collaborate. The best teams also call out poor behaviour very quickly, and there is no allowance, even for the best performers. Finally, no one makes excuses for poor performance.

If I got the call tomorrow to lead a team, these are the lessons I'd follow. I've always thought that the ultimate test of culture in a sporting environment is this. Could a new signing come and watch a team train and know what the cultural dynamics of that team were at the end of a session? If I were to walk into the Liverpool dressing room right now before the start of any game, I bet I'd witness most of the things I've just outlined. I don't work at Liverpool, but you can smell high-functioning culture from a distance. I had the same feeling about Paul McGinley's team in his Ryder Cup triumph.

The cultural dynamics of a sporting environment are crucial to success, and I have learned a great deal over the years because I've witnessed the good, the bad and the ugly. As our company has grown and as I've been around more businesses and talked to many more people, I've learned much more about the framework to drive fantastic culture. Much of that has informed how my company behaves today, so I'm going to share a few key examples and a few key things I've learned along the way.

Everyone will always cite Google in the context of company culture, and it's certainly true that they're among the best at it. What I like about their cultural framework though is their 'Ten things we know to be true'. It's an excellent guide for anyone working there and anyone, like me, just interested in how to build the right culture. Here they are:

Focus on the user, and all else will follow
It's best to do one thing really, really well
Fast is better than slow
Democracy on the web works

> You don't need to be at your desk to need an answer
> You can make money without doing evil
> There's always more information out there
> The need for information crosses all borders
> You can be serious without a suit
> Great just isn't good enough

I like these but most of all, I like the principle behind them. In the context of culture and overall team performance, here are some things I know to be true;

> It's better to ask for forgiveness than permission
> Make shit happen
> The customer is king and queen
> Seven out of ten right decisions in a week is a good week
> You need to give something back every day
> If you've got a problem with someone, look to yourself to work out why
> The point about bullshit is that you can smell it a mile away
> If it's not fun, it's not worth it
> Nothing is impossible

You don't have to know the answer
But it's good to know the person who does

I might add another which is, 'You can be serious in a pair of flip flops.' For those who know me well, they will understand this!

I love Netflix. I love the product, and I love what it does; it's has been lauded globally for how it has built a culture around its employees. Their focus is all about output, not input. In other words, no one judges people by the hours that they spend at work, more the work that they've achieved. In doing so, they are asking their people to be accountable and responsible, and it works; this is an issue that I've grappled with over the years. I know myself well enough to know that I'm a control freak, and sometimes that's at odds with letting teams steer their destiny. Instinctively for years, I've known that I needed to get better at this. Two years ago, I finally bit the bullet, let go and hired a group CEO, Jonathan Douglas or JD as he's known. He introduced things I'd never heard of and frankly was not interested in. One day he suggested to me that we should invest in a new finance software package called Sage. I agreed although until that point in my life, I thought Sage was something you had with your Sunday lunch. Having JD at the helm has been the best and hardest thing I've done. We urgently needed to move from a lifestyle business to one that grew up. I knew I couldn't do that, and I was lucky to find the person that could help me.

I love Zappos too. They are relentless about creating the right culture. Their hiring process starts with a cultural fit interview which carries significant weight over whether to hire someone. Here's the best thing of all. Their CEO, Tony Hsieh, offers employees money to quit after their first few weeks if they don't feel that they are the right fit for the business. They say that a principle isn't a principle until it costs you money. There's a great example of that. Finally, our company works hard to make sure that all of our teams have the chance to spend time together socially. I think it's essential. Warby Parker, the online prescription glasses site in the US make sure that there's always an upcoming event, so the entire team has something exciting ahead. It also selects random employees to go out to lunch together, which strikes me as a great idea. I'm not sure how many people would like to draw me if we did that so we might give that one a miss! Just a few examples then from companies I've met and researched as I've tried to work out how to build our culture. We are not perfect by any stretch of the imagination. However, we are continually finding ways of creating the kind of culture that we can all be proud of and which respects every single member of our team.

Many years ago, I remembered hearing people talk about someone's work-life balance, and I also remember thinking what a load of old guff that was. People just don't think like that. There's no such thing as your work and your life. Just your life of which work is a part. I'm more aware than ever before of the need to make that bit of everyone's life at D&G called work as rewarding and as engaging as I possibly can. I know how influential culture is to that process. I only wish everyone I played with and was coached by over the years had realised that.

Chapter Nine

Honesty is Always the Best Policy

AT ITS best, cricket is a game full of passion, skill, integrity, character and sporting behaviour of the highest order. On 24 March 2018, many of those ideals disappeared in front of a worldwide audience. The Aussies were touring South Africa, and after lunch on the third day of the third Test match, Cameron Bancroft suddenly found himself in the spotlight for all the wrong reasons. On television coverage around the world and screens at the ground, he was caught rubbing the ball with a small yellow object. Minutes after Bancroft got wind that there was a problem, he tried to hide the object down the front of his trousers. The umpires approached him to work out what was going on. Bancroft then showed them a dark sunglasses pouch. The rest of the story is history. Suffice to say, lie followed lie. Five days later, Bancroft admitted that he had used sandpaper on the ball with the full knowledge of both the captain and vice-captain of the Aussie team. Worse still, it emerged very quickly that the leadership duo had asked Bancroft to do it. As I write the detail of this Aussie horror story, I still can't quite believe it happened, but it did. Much of what lies at the heart of that story is the subject of this chapter. Honesty, integrity and why sport and business will always find you out if you don't play it with a straight bat.

Much has been said and written about sandpaper-gate. Despite that, not enough has been written about two crucial aspects of that incident. Firstly, it demonstrated that culturally, the Australia cricket team at the time was rotten to the core. The incident itself was not the worst thing about it. The most insidious aspect of it was that the two senior leaders of the team had asked the most junior team member to execute the plan. If you're going to cheat boys, at least have the guts to do it yourselves. In many ways, I had some sympathy for Bancroft at the time. How many players desperate to keep their place in the national side would say no to their leaders? And there lies the second real issue with the Aussie side at that time. No one felt that they could explain to Smith or Warner that their plan violated every law and code of conduct in the game and was a ridiculously toxic idea. From that, you can deduce that the players didn't question Smith or Warner about anything. Every single member of the Aussie side was frightened of Smith and Warner and the influence they had. I've witnessed that kind of issue in a changing room (and a business) before and it's debilitating and corrosive. Since leaving the game and having the responsibility of building a business and looking after people, I've realised that there's a thing called psychological safety. Without it, any team is toast just as the Aussies demonstrated. Not for the first time, something that I had experienced in sport had a direct correlation to the business I was building.

You're in a room with six other colleagues, and your boss has asked for an update on the week's events. One of the team starts describing a meeting you were in earlier in the week. The detail of that meeting is relayed inaccurately to avoid an awkward conversation in the room. You know the client didn't like the pitch, and you know that there's a good reason for the boss to get involved. Do you say anything, or do you let your colleague continue to gloss over the issue? The team is chasing 350, and you are now three wickets down.

The captain, who has just got out, storms into the changing room claiming that no one is going to be able to get runs on that pitch. You know that the six batsmen left to go in have all heard this. Do you speak up and suggest to the captain that this may not be the most helpful intervention, or do you say nothing for fear of being dropped for the next game? If the answer in both cases is no, you've got your first clue that you are in an environment that has no psychological safety.

I love TED talks. For those of you not familiar with them, TED is a non-profit organisation whose aim is to spread ideas through short, powerful talks. There are thousands of them on the web. I first came across the concept of psychological safety during one of these talks, and it immediately resonated with me. Amy Edmondson, the Harvard Business School Professor of Leadership and Management, did lots of comparative research on different teams and their effectiveness. The data she gathered was unequivocal but counter-intuitive; better teams were making more mistakes. After further work, she realised that better teams were not making more mistakes. They were just communicating more openly and more honestly about making them. That's when she coined the phrase 'psychological safety' and defined it as follows:

'Psychological safety means that team members feel safe to take risks and be vulnerable in front of each other.'

I remember the day I watched that talk, and I felt energised and angry in equal measure. Energised because I had found a way of framing what I instinctively knew to be right about life and the business. I was also angry because I realised that I had grown up in a sporting environment that was, at times, psychologically very unsafe. My feelings of despair and depression as a cricketer had been driven by not being able to be vulnerable. I'll never forget the conversation with the doctor the first time I discussed my anxieties. 'Drink more water' was the advice; what a joke. In my world, growing up in cricket, being vulnerable was seen as a weakness and never discussed. I was so pleased when Jonathan Trott, Marcus Trescothick and Freddie Flintoff all talked about their anxieties both during and after their careers. It raised the profile of this issue immensely. If players that talented and successful were suffering, I wonder how many blokes that I played with were also suffering? I now know that 'it's okay not to be okay'. This phrase is now widely used in discussions about mental health. I think it helps everyone understand why it's so important to be open and honest about how you're feeling.

It makes me angry now to think about the very many times that I suffered at the hands of bullying coaches. I have a considerable fear too that, for all the talk and bluster sport, in general, hasn't moved on fast enough or intelligently enough in this area. I wonder how many cricketers at Middlesex, for example, feel truly psychologically safe. I only use my county as a reference point because everyone knows that's my club, not because I necessarily think there's an issue there. Only the players know that. Only they know whether they have the right outlets to maintain their levels of mental well-being and if the players don't, whether or not they can say so. I've long wondered whether I should use my own experience as a cricketer to campaign for better mental well-being provision in sport generally. If it weren't such an urgent issue, I'd put it on the 'to do' list for retirement.

Once I understood the concept of psychological safety, I realised very quickly that who is on a team matters far less than how they interact and work together. Of course, one of the significant issues here is that people in groups are reluctant to engage in behaviour that could negatively influence how others view them, either in terms of their abilities or how they feel about their environment. That's why this concept is so vital in building the right culture in your business. It's worth saying at this juncture that you know when you have a psychologically safe relationship. I'm lucky to have one with my family, but over the years, I'm also fortunate to have had them with people close to me, including my clients.

One that stands out is Peter Aldis, who ran Holland & Barrett very successfully. In many ways, Peter and I are cut from the same 'no-nonsense' cloth. He's better looking and more talented than me but fortunately used to come a very poor second in the drinking stakes, so I liked going out for a beer with him. On a more serious note, Peter taught me a considerable amount about an approach to business that cuts through the bullshit. He made honesty the only thing that mattered in our day-to-day dealings. It was a real joy having him as a client. Here was a man who led Holland & Barrett to 39 quarters of consecutive growth which is an extraordinary achievement. I remember one day going to the Nuneaton head office to see the client team before our first Holland & Barrett event. As I was walking through the building with everyone, Peter saw me and came over. Before I could say anything, Peter said to me in a thunderous voice, 'Nashy, whatever you do, don't f*** up my golf day,' and walked away. My team were a bit shocked, but it didn't surprise me. Peter Aldis took no prisoners, and you always knew where you stood with him. He is my kind of client.

I've always tried to build psychological safety into my teams, into my business and my relationships. I've done this in three ways. Firstly, it's hugely important to think of work as a learning opportunity and to be completely accepting of mistakes. Allowing everyone to make those mistakes and creating opportunities for real learning is critical. Secondly, everyone (including the leadership group) has to acknowledge that they are not perfect openly. In my experience, people respond well to other people displaying their fallibility. Finally, you need to build a culture in your business in which curiosity and questioning matter more than anything else. I've learned over the years that the more people question what I'm doing, the more I learn, and the better my ideas become. I want people in my business who are two things; interesting and interested.

There's then a secret magic ingredient that is an extraordinary sauce indeed, and that's honesty and the ability to go beyond the superficial. How many times has someone asked how you are, for you to reply, 'Fine, thanks,' even though you're not? How many times do you have a meaningful conversation with a work colleague that goes beyond the superficial? How much do you know about the guy in your team who opens the batting with you? Or the person that you have to travel to Hull with every week? Not as much as you should, I'd argue. You see, the thing about real psychological safety in teams is that you can't achieve it unless you move beyond the superficial. People simply won't display their fallibility or vulnerability unless they are in a relationship of mutual trust and understanding. It's up to you to make that happen, and if you do, you'll be amazed at the difference it makes. In the end, you have to bring the real version of you into the workplace to achieve this, and that's hard. This issue is my next topic.

For those of you who know me well, sit down and pour yourself a drink because I'm about to quote Shakespeare. In case Stuart Law is reading this, Shakespeare was one of our greatest poets and playwrights and probably the world's greatest dramatist. Stuart's Australian so won't know that.

Our greatest ever playwright wrote the following immortal words:

'To thine own self be true, and it must follow, as the night the day, thou canst not then be false to any man.'

I think I'd have got outstanding odds on Shakespeare appearing in my book. But he has, and the reason is simple.

Being true to yourself is one of the very best things you can do throughout the whole of your life. I should know because it has worked for me. I've never really pretended to be anything other than who I am, and people have responded to that, I think. They know that I'm straight up and they know that I tell it as it is. It's always been my way, and I respond best to people who are like that too. I worry about people who try and be something that they're not, not least because that's a sure sign that they are not happy with who they are. It's a continuation of this theme of psychological safety. The more honest you are with yourself and with others, the more likely you are to be in teams where that is true. I don't think individuals can grow unless they're honest with themselves about where they are today and where they want to be tomorrow. The issue in business generally and even our business specifically is that it's all too easy to hide sometimes. Behind your boss, behind the economy, behind a problematic client or behind the product or service you're offering. Most of the time, it's nonsense, and it's an example of people not being honest with themselves.

For all its issues, one of the things I love about sport is that there are no hiding places. Your batting averages speak for themselves; Lewis Hamilton's track times are in black and white; England do or don't win the penalty shoot-out. I think this is one of the many reasons why sportsmen and women make excellent business leaders. Not just because of the lessons aplenty from sport that relate to business but because they have become accustomed to being honest about themselves and their performance. In professional sport, there is no other way. The more measurable the environment, the more honest you have to be.

One of the most honest men in football today is Sean Dyche. He's someone I know well and someone I've admired from a distance for many years. Getting to know him has given me some fascinating insights into his leadership style and his belief in how teams perform best. One of Sean's mantras is about clarity of information being the catalyst to allow you to develop real clarity of thought. I liked that thought the very first time I heard it. One of Sean's early decisions, when he arrived at Burnley, was to allow his players to answer (anonymously) a straightforward set of questions. Those questions allowed them to assess the club, where they were as individuals and how the club could best move forward. It was a sign that Burnley had got a new manager who not only wanted to listen to his new players – he knew that the best way to build trust quickly was to create an open and honest environment in which all of the potential issues were out in the open. In that way, Sean Dyche and Andrew Strauss are cut from the same leadership cloth.

I've tried to avoid almost any part of this book becoming a self-help manual. However, this chapter finishes with observations on bringing the best version of yourself to any situation, be that work or sport. Some of these have worked for me and some of these I've seen work for other people. There's a reason we have two ears and one mouth, and that's because it's the proportion we need to use them. Listen more, talk less, it's incredible how much you'll learn and how much people will value being around you. Someone much wiser than me once told me that there are two types of people in this regard. People who genuinely hear what people are saying and people who are only listening, so they know when to start talking. So many of us know both kinds of people. Never worry about improving your weaknesses. Just spend time making the strengths you have even better. They are called super strengths, and improving those will make you an incredibly valuable member of the team. That way of thinking will also free you up from the tyranny of the outdated appraisal and the need to be good at everything. I've got some news for you. No one is good at everything, and no one needs to be. There are so many things I can't do.

I can't drive, I can't cook, I'm a comical novice with technology, and I'm useless at DIY. When I was younger, my mum used to pack my bags for my Middlesex games and label each day's clothes in plastic bags. When the lads saw this, you can imagine their reaction. I quickly had to tell my mum to drop the labels. I was a mummy's boy par excellence in those days. Jules would say that I still am.

Finally, I have a piece of advice I've offered up already in this book, but it's an important one. Go out of your way to celebrate other people's success. The more you do that, the more other people will celebrate yours, and the better you'll feel about yourself. It's the ultimate win-win. Psychological safety matters; it matters in sport, it makes businesses work better, and it allows people to thrive. It can only ever happen in environments where people are honest, want to learn and feel safe to express their opinion. I've been in situations where there's been no safety, and it's soul-destroying. If I had one real regret in my cricket career, it's that I wished I had spoken up earlier.

Chapter Ten

'No Man is an Island'

ONE OF them scored 41,112 first-class runs and hit 136 centuries. The other scored 35,659 runs with 114 centuries. Between them though, they only managed just over 5,500 runs and eight centuries in Test matches. They were two of the finest players I ever watched while playing the game. They were also two players (of quite a few actually) who, when I watched them, made me realise just how far away I was from international honours. In both cases, neither translated their prodigious talent from the county stage to the international one. There has been much speculation over the years in cricketing circles as to why. I'm going to add to that body of opinion in this chapter. I'm writing, of course, about Mark Ramprakash and Graeme Hick. Fantastic cricketers and imposing men. They were enigmatic, intense, and both had insecurities that were perceived as aloofness. This wasn't true, but sometimes, perception is reality.

It would be hard to meet a more committed, driven cricketer than Ramps was. His nickname was Bloodaxe, a reference to his short temper, something to which the showers at the Oval (which he demolished once) will testify. Thinking about Ramps and showers reminds me of a story at Trent Bridge. I did the worst thing you could to Ramps during one game in particular; I ran him out. Shortly afterwards, I got out myself and so walked into the dressing room very nervously waiting for Ramps to confront me. He was nowhere to be seen, thankfully. After I'd taken my pads off, I went to the loo just to gather my thoughts. There, I was greeted with a sight I'll never forget. The lunatic Ramps was lying in the bath in his full kit including spikes, pads and helmet, just chuntering to himself about what an arsehole I was. I exited that toilet as fast as humanly possible! In the case of both Ramps and Hicky, I think they could have benefited from one more thing in their locker, and it's the subject of this chapter – mentors. The role mentors play in your life. In this regard, I learned something from cricket that has helped me understand how to improve consistently.

For Ramps and Hick, I think it was all too easy for them to go into their respective shells and not talk about their fears, their goals and their state of mind. They were two huge players in their day and probably so big that lots of people didn't want to approach them. Ramps's form for England certainly picked up after a spell chatting to Steve Bull, the England psychologist, but it wasn't consistent. My hunch is that, in both Ramps and Hicky's case, broader access to a more open mentor network would have helped their careers immensely. More open dialogue, more honest dialogue and helping them both to overcome their visible cricketing demons. I hope one or both of them read this book and come for a beer with me at some point. I'd love to know if my hunch is right. So, in this chapter, I'm going to explore what a mentor is and should be. I want to examine what their role is and how sport can give you a head start in understanding how to develop yourself in business and life.

I remember the first time I decided to take the plunge and become an entrepreneur. I say become one, but I'd been doing entrepreneurial things for some time before D&G was born, as I've already explained. As a cricketer getting towards the end of his career, you have to start to think of ways of making extra pie and mash. I was excited to go it alone with my brother and asked lots of people for advice about the business, the business model and how I should go about building D&G. I had incredible support, and it's not until I look back on all the advice I received and used over the years that I've realised that mentors help in all sorts of ways.

At their best, mentors provide information and knowledge. In the words of Benjamin Franklin:

'Tell me, and I forget. Teach me, and I may remember. Involve me, and I learn.'

That quote resonates with me because it's how I learn. When you start a business, you're pretty clueless about a great deal of the day-to-day business of running a business. Business plans, cash flow, marketing, budgeting, how to balance the urgent and important are all new. You have to rely on people with a wealth of knowledge in that area to help speed up your learning curve. One of the other things that good mentors do, of course, is to spot things that you wouldn't recognise yourself. A good mentor doesn't blow your tyres up. They are there to tell you exactly how it is, and you have to be prepared to listen and accept their advice and opinion. It has to be a two-way street.

I've seen lots of mentor/mentee relationships. Some of the best I've witnessed occur when mentors find exciting ways to help fuel others' personal and professional growth. It's quite often about smart goal setting and the constant monitoring of those goals with regular check-ins. It could be about launching a new group within the company or testing a new approach to new business. The point is that great mentors observe processes like that and make suggestions about ways to improve throughout the process. In these kinds of relationships, you'll also find that there's lots of conversation around character and values. I've seen people get it spectacularly wrong. I've mentioned John Buchanan before, and any coach should be part-coach, part mentor to the players. The coach must understand the character and motivation of each of his players. With Mark Ramprakash, he often had a shocker. Before every new game, John would analyse our previous game in detail to help identify ways in which we could improve. One tool he used was the wagon wheel, which is the chart in cricket that shows where each of your scoring shots went in the ground. I remember in this particular review session that I'd got nought and one across two innings. So, my only line was the single run I'd nurdled down to fine leg. Worse was to come though when Ramps got his wagon wheel from the two ducks he'd had that game. All that was on the card were two stumps and a boundary rope. Ramps was a fiery character as I've already explained. He was furious and stormed out that day, leaving John Buchanan in no doubt that he thought our coach was a complete joke. Theirs was a mentor/mentee relationship that never worked.

I don't often quote Oprah Winfrey, but on this occasion, it's worth it. I came across something she once said, and it stayed with me. 'A mentor is someone who allows you to see the hope inside yourself.' Not the kind of thing quoted in the changing rooms I used to be in, to be honest. But the point here is that a brilliant mentor knows that their role is to provide guidance and encouragement. I have suffered my fair share of anxieties over the years, and this encouragement has been vital in that context. To go back to something I mentioned earlier, I often wonder how much help stars like Hicky and Ramps got and how much more prolific they might have been if they'd had that. Who knows?

In many ways and on some occasions, mentors behave in similar ways to how your parents used to act. I'm someone who occasionally benefits from a bit of tough love, and I certainly get it from my family. Mentors are disciplinarians, and they create boundaries. That's important particularly for entrepreneurs because self-motivation and self-discipline can sometimes be challenging when lots of other things are going on around you. I know this from my own experience. If I'm feeling low, my self-discipline goes out of the window, and I dive into the chocolate. Mentors teach you good disciplines, and they remind you to maintain those disciplines as well.

I'm an ideas man. I love them, and I have lots of them. I'm always thinking of ways in which we can own more of our supply chain, set up new businesses and build closer relationships with the clients we have. It's why we started our silent auction business, for example. I saw what others did, and I knew that we could do it better and more creatively. To go back to an earlier chapter; with a bit of *kaizen*, it's incredible how often you can improve what's already there. However, mentors have a vital role to play in this process as sounding boards and good filters.

I've had quite a few poor ideas knocked back over the years, saving myself a great deal of money and pain in the process. I'm not someone who trusts people easily. Quite the opposite. I'm very untrusting of most things. It's one of the reasons why I check our business bank account every day. You just never know. Your ideal mentor is someone who has no stake in any idea or business of yours so that they can give you genuinely objective advice. Mentors should also be one of your best networking avenues, and they should draw on their mistakes and not let you make the same ones. I'm fortunate in both of my careers to have had great mentors, and they've made an enormous difference to my progress. But it was professional sport that gave me an invaluable grounding in understanding the role of mentors. I can tell you that I think most people in business get it wrong. Let me explain.

Professional cricket and indeed professional sport generally have vast numbers of specialist coaches, doctors, support staff and advisors. You only have to look at the way that the European Ryder Cup team has developed over the years to see the point I'm making. We will soon be at the stage where there are as many vice-captains as there are players. I'm not criticising that at any level for reasons that will become obvious. Nowadays, cricket teams have batting, bowling and fielding coaches. Top football teams have attacking, defending and goalkeeping coaches. Every major sports team has at least one psychologist, a dietician and an army of physios. The point is not the number of people but the variety. Every team needs very different guidance from very different individuals at any one time. The Ryder Cup assistant coaches all have a range of experience that they can impart at certain times during the three days.

They also, inevitably, have different personalities. One of the key ingredients to a successful Ryder Cup is to match the characters of the vice-captains with the players. If you're Ian Poulter, you need a different type of mentor for the week than Henrik Stenson. This approach is your classic marginal gain, something that I wrote about earlier. You need a different mindset in foursomes to singles, for example. Great teams understand this, and they also know that the quality and variety of expertise that surrounds the players is key to success.

In his recent book, *Rebel Ideas*, Matthew Syed has written about this very thing. It's a great read and makes the point that the most crucial diversity that any team can have isn't based on gender, age or race. It's about what he calls cognitive diversity; the need to have people who think very differently to achieve great results.

John Buchanan was the Middlesex coach in the 1998 season and was a man who thought differently. Much has been written about his record in cricket. Ricky Ponting credits Buchanan with being one of the main reasons that Australia won three World Cups. Shane Warne, on the other hand, believes that Buchanan simply reinvented everything for the sake of it and complicated almost every aspect of the game. Whatever the truth, I certainly witnessed his attempt at building cognitive diversity into our changing room. His view was that no one player was 'bigger than the game'. He had the youngsters rooming with the older players to promote more shared learnings and got rid of the second XI changing room. In his view, it was divisive. The result? He lasted no time in the job because the senior players hated his approach, and he lost the dressing room very early on. As I reflect on this period in my career, it's a great lesson in making sure that you get buy-in from the top before you instigate any significant change. You can attempt to build as much cognitive diversity as you want. But, unless you bring everyone with you, it will always fail.

I still remember the value of having several different people to guide me through the early stages of my cricket career. They had varying levels of experience and unique perspectives on how I should go about things. Frank Sharman was a Sunbury legend and someone who helped me massively. He was a big man in every sense of the word. A tall, imposing figure who always had my back. He also always had time for me and everyone else around him. One of my real regrets revolves around Frank. He became ill sometime before Sunbury played Sandiacre Town in the

National Club Final in 2015. We lost that final by a couple of wickets which should not have happened. It was a game we should have won. I wanted to win that day for big Frank who is, very sadly, no longer with us. He is a man who will always hold a special place in my heart.

Richard Johnson (Jonno to his mates) was a very talented cricketer and one of my closest team-mates at Middlesex. He is now forging a great career as a coach. In many ways, Jonno is the reason that I had a cricket career that lasted as long as it did. In those early days, it was tough. I've talked about what it was like living at home. The pressure of coming home to Mum and Dad, the two people who cared about me and my cricket more than anyone in the whole world, was mentally debilitating. That pressure got to me, and so, Jonno offering me a room at his place was a game-changer for me. He wasn't just my landlord, however, and that's mainly because I didn't pay him. He was someone I looked up to and someone who helped me through the dark times back then. He still does. In those early days, he was like a father figure to me. I've got to be honest and say that I didn't always behave that well. Late nights, too much alcohol and some poor behaviour all meant that Jonno had to have the patience of a saint, which he did (most of the time). I was a handful in those days, but Jonno took me under his wing and guided me through the ups and downs. For that, and his ongoing close friendship, I will be eternally grateful.

Let's now look at how lots of businesspeople engage with mentors. Often, and indeed in most cases, it's one person. Their coach, their mentor, their advisor all wrapped up in one; a person with one set of experiences and one approach. It's no wonder so many people fail to develop in the way that they'd like. It's a wholly inadequate way of doing it. I'd argue for a whole new approach to the way you think about mentors, and it's something that's served me well over the last few years. When thinking about who your mentor should be, don't think about one person but think about a team of people to support you, all with different skills and opinions. Use the power of the way sports teams approach these things to build your mentor matrix. Like ADAM earlier, I reckon I should trademark the mentor matrix! What is it? Five people, all of whom have something different to offer. So, let's look at who they should be.

Firstly, you need an industry expert; a person who knows business and preferably your sector backwards. For me, that was John King. He was retail through and through, and retail clients were our bread and butter. They can provide insight into the industry you're in, and they are your 'go-to' person for anything business-related.

Secondly, you need a cheerleader. Not the ones with pompoms but someone who you know is talking you and your business up at all times. Mike Tobin has always been that in our company. If you're the leader of an organisation, you need people to do this externally. If you're in a team, find someone who can sing your praises internally. They are your PR machine and your best connectors within the company and to the outside world.

Thirdly, you need a plus one, a co-pilot, a partner in crime or in my case a brother called Glen. This co-pilot will often be someone at your level in the company or one of your business partners. Still, their role is (and yours is with theirs) to support, collaborate and hold each other responsible.

To build the matrix properly, you also need a rock; someone who knows you well and has your best interests at heart outside of the business. It's the person to whom you can reveal your innermost fears but also the person for whom no subject is off-limits, personal or professional. I'm lucky to have Jules for all of those things.

Finally, you need a wild card. Everyone assumes that your mentor has to be older than you. Why? Nowadays, people younger than me are tech billionaires. Or choose someone as your wild card who you know is so argumentative that they are going to disagree with you come what may. Or, make it someone new every month that you barely know. Either way, the wild card is there to give you something very different and to keep you on your toes. In our business, Adam did this in abundance. Not the ADAM model I discussed earlier but my ex-business partner Adam Stanier. He was argumentative and very annoying sometimes. Still, he always gave me a different perspective which has been invaluable over the years. He was a fantastic partner with whom to start our business because he did some things brilliantly that I just can't do.

I often talk about finding, binding and grinding when it comes to business. You need someone who is a new business whirlwind (a finder), and I guess that's me in our company. But then, you also need someone who can bind the client into the company; contracts, processes and making sure that we never drop the ball. Adam was a great binder; he is one of the best. He'll be happy with that I'm sure; not least because I haven't called him a grinder! I'll reserve that role for my brother Glen. A man who is the antithesis of me in almost every way. So much so that I often wonder if we are brothers. He's super-organised, loves detail and has more files than WH Smith! He's a man who gets the job done and I'd trust him with my life.

So, that's my mentor matrix, driven by my experience in sport but now framed as a piece of advice for any young person or entrepreneur starting up. Think very carefully about the people that you choose to help you. It can't be one person because if it is, your learning opportunities are minimal. Think of my matrix and build a team around you who can give you the right things at the right time. That's what great teams in sport and business do.

At this stage of the book, I get to freestyle for a paragraph. I'm going to assume that for the next few minutes, I'm mentoring you (alongside the other four legends in the matrix of course). I've no idea who you are, and I've no idea what you do, but I'm going to imagine that we have an initial chat. I'd be making sure that you have a plan and a focus around the following: Do you know why work and your job matters to you? I referred to this earlier in the book as purpose. Still, it's perhaps the most fundamental thing you need to understand about your job and career. Are you happy that you are being recognised and rewarded for the work that you do? If you are, that's a short conversation. If you're not, I'd want to help you make a plan for getting to that point. Thirdly, are you progressing; in terms of your role and the skills you want to develop? Do you feel that the people above you notice the contribution you make and do you feel challenged in the job you have? It's important to feel challenged every day by your role because that's the only way that you will grow. Finally, and perhaps most importantly, do you feel in control of your destiny? Are there any significant obstacles, human or otherwise, in your job that interfere with how happy you are? Is there anything preventing you from doing your job or progressing quickly? These questions are the most important for any mentor. If you care about your career as much as you should, make sure you find a group of people who can help you progress in each of the crucial areas. By all means, give me a bell, by the way. I'd be happy to help. I'm going to write about what my future may hold in the very final chapter. For now, if any young entrepreneurs are reading this who need money or expertise in getting to the next level, call me. In case you think that's not a serious offer, my number is 07768 558086.

So, the question of mentors is an interesting one. I think lots of people get it wrong. I'd argue that, without them, you are giving yourself a much bigger hill to climb in your life and your business. The answer, though, doesn't lie in one person. How could it? The answer has to lie in you choosing a group of people, all of whom have the right background and skillset to help. If you do that and you work your nuts off, you'll smash it.

Chapter Eleven

That Which Can't Be Measured Never Gets Done

LORD KELVIN, a physicist of some repute centuries ago (although I'd never heard of him either), once offered up the following pearl of wisdom:

> I often say that when you can measure what you are speaking about, and express it in numbers, you know something about it; but when you cannot measure it, when you cannot express it in numbers, your knowledge is of a meagre and unsatisfactory kind.

He's right, of course, and put another way, numbers rule the world. There's one for my finance director. There is not a sport on the planet like cricket where this matters more. Numbers drive the game: averages, records in numbers, and numerical analysis. However, I've also seen countless examples, particularly in selection, where a reliance on the numbers ignores talent and gut instinct. Too often, I've seen people in cricket and business hide behind the numbers to justify poor decisions. Numbers must only ever act as a guide, not as a final decision-maker.

I mentioned my love of Brentford earlier in this book. Beyond my passion for the team, I'm fascinated by the Brentford story and its relevance to numbers. As I write this, the club is regularly pushing for top-flight football. Regardless of whether they achieve that goal in the years to come, the club is on the up. This success is all driven by Thomas Frank, the manager, and Matthew Benham, the owner. Benham made his millions from professional gambling, and he loves his numbers; a topic which I'll come back to later in the book. Brentford deploy the so-called 'Moneyball' strategy; the hugely successful, data-driven method of selecting players that served the Oakland Athletics baseball team so well. This strategy has made Brentford money, improved their football and in doing so, has allowed them to grow commercially. A new ground now also heralds a new era for Brentford fans everywhere.

The commercial engine at Brentford is the responsibility of a good mate of mine, Jon Varney, the CEO. His mates call him Reg though after the unforgettable Reg Varney from TV sitcom *On the Buses*. When I compare Brentford's approach to how most English cricket clubs behave, it is night and day. If only Middlesex used the 'Moneyball' strategy to find batsmen who consistently make runs on the kind of surface we have at Lord's. That kind of approach would be a game-changer. Maybe I'll try and set up a meeting with Matthew Benham and the Middlesex board after this book is out.

Never were the numbers more to the fore than in the 1992 World Cup semi-final between England and South Africa. Here a method of analysing how you calculate runs needed versus time left in the game in the event of a stoppage in play caused havoc. It was known as the most productive overs method. Rain stopped play for 12 minutes with South Africa needing 22 runs from 13 balls. The revised target left South Africa needing 21 runs from one ball, a reduction of only one run compared to a decrease of two overs. It was an impossible target and the nail in the coffin for the most productive overs method.

Enter two statisticians, Frank Duckworth and Tony Lewis. They saw the opportunity to build a much more robust model for this sort of eventuality. The Duckworth-Lewis method was born and has been an ever-present part of the game since that infamous semi-final. It's also got plenty of comic value for all of us cricket lovers because of its complexity and because there's almost no one in the game who understands it. As a spectator, and more importantly, as a team, you just know it gives you an exact guide as to where your scoring rate should be if the heavens open or the light fades.

Well, that's true unless your name is John Emburey. Embers is a brilliant bloke, and I enjoyed playing with him hugely when he was my captain. Sadly, he was no expert on Duckworth-Lewis. I remember many a time when a crumpled piece of paper would be passed from him to the team. On it, he explained what our runs and wickets total needed to be at the end of a particular over. The problem was that it was never right. Either Embers wasn't great at maths or, like the rest of us when it comes to Duckworth-Lewis in those days, he was just making it up!

In case anyone is interested, I've always thought of Duckworth-Lewis as a statistical model whose essence is resources. Each team is assumed to have two 'resources' to use to score as many runs as possible: the number of overs they have to receive and the number of wickets they have in hand. At any point in the innings, a team's ability to score more runs depends on the combination of these two remaining resources. That's it, in a nutshell, but don't ask me to write down the formula! Duckworth-Lewis was a significant innovation in the game of cricket. It moved cricket on, and it's all about the analysis of numbers as so much of cricket is.

While we are on the subject of innovation (of which Duckworth-Lewis is a great example), here is a small aside and a bee that is often in my bonnet. The words creativity and innovation are often bandied around in business to demonstrate progress, to show why a company is different and how it thinks laterally. Very often, the terms are interchangeable and are used to mean the same thing. That's wrong. The two things are very different, and we use them very differently in our business.

Both words are hugely important, but both have distinct and different roles to play in driving change. Innovation is the process by which you make something that's already there, much better: a process, a product or a piece of marketing, for example. Creativity is the art of coming up with something genuinely original. It's arguably the hardest thing to do which is why top talent in that world gets paid top dollar. The most impressive people I've met in my business life are those that are continually seeking to innovate and create and don't mind failing in the process.

Let me give you a very personal example. When we were starting our business, I used to meet lots of people who gave me lots of business cards. I had lots of conversations, and it was tough for me to see the wood for the trees. It was almost impossible to follow up with many of them in a meaningful way. So, I thought long and hard about how to do it differently. I changed the way I went about it and decided to grab five minutes to myself after chatting to anyone who had given me their business card. Immediately after the conversation, I'd write something down on the back of the business card. This might be the name of their partner and children (if they'd mentioned it) or something unique to them that had come up in the conversation. That way, I was able to break the ice in the follow-up call or note with a question that was all about them. It made a difference because it showed that I was genuinely interested in them as a person first and foremost, and it gave me the confidence to make the call. I haven't blown my own trumpet much in this book, so you'll forgive me for doing it now. That change (or piece of innovation) around new business follow-ups made a more significant difference to our conversion rate than anything else in our early years. It was also crucial for another reason, which was that it allowed me to establish real relationships with people much more quickly. Given that it is one of my key strengths in business, it did have a considerable benefit.

Let's get back to the numbers. As I said at the very beginning of this book, I was pretty average as a professional cricketer, and my stats are a testament to that. Given this is a chapter on numbers, it would be remiss of me not to include mine for you to judge for yourself. I played 140 first-class matches and scored 5,684 runs at an average of 35.52. I scored 11 hundreds and 27 half-centuries. My top score was 114. Some 297 catches and 23 stumpings later, I hung up my boots in first-class cricket. Looking back on those numbers now, I'd make two observations, and this would be the chat I'd have with my 20-year-old self. I scored a ton on 11 occasions but never got beyond 114. That's poor and in all honesty, still pisses me off. As anyone who knows cricket will tell you, as a batsman, once you're in you need to make the most of it and convert those hundreds into what the great Graham Gooch used to call 'Daddy hundreds'. Of course, had I converted a few of those, my average would have been much better. Goochy played a role in our business for a while, given that some of our prospective clients loved cricket. When we did pitch together, he was the G in D&G, which was a neat pivot. His mere presence helped us get a few clients over the line. He was also our driver to meetings since I can't drive. On a trip up to Manchester once, he did remark that, given his glittering career, he hadn't ever imagined that, one day, he'd be driving me around! I love it.

My second observation about my numbers would be a positive one. Not many people have the privilege of playing professional sport. I'm now more grateful than ever for the career that I had and the times when I did enjoy it. It was tough along the way as I've explained, but I look back with a tremendous amount of pride that I played at a decent level for so long. There's a big part of me that wishes I had enjoyed it more and been much bolder. The coaches pigeon-holed me at Middlesex as a 'nudger and nurdler'.The kind of batsman who scored slowly but effectively and was told to do that. Looking back now, I wished I'd ignored that, been my own man and been much more expansive at the crease. I also wish I'd stopped to smell the flowers more, as they say. That's good advice generally for any young person reading this.

Whatever you do, enjoy the journey and live in the present. Someone much wiser than me once drew me a picture of a mountain with lots of peaks along the way. He was trying to illustrate that people approach life in two different ways. Some scale the first peak and immediately look up and think, 'Blimey, that's a long way to go.' Others look down and enjoy the view for ten minutes before embarking on the next stage of the journey. I try to remind myself every day to enjoy the view a bit more. If nothing else, it does wonders for my well-being.

Cricket is a game of numbers then, and over the years, there have been some iconic ones. The number 99.94 and the legendary Sir Donald George Bradman will, forever, be linked. Some would say that 99.94 represents the most significant achievement by any sportsman in any major sport. The Don was a man who would practise alone with only a cricket stump and a golf ball growing up. In the words of the former Australian captain, Bill Woodfull, Bradman was 'worth three batsmen to Australia'. In his final ever innings, The Don, as he became known, needed just four runs to ensure a career Test average of 100. He was out for a duck so was stuck on only 99.94. Just three times my career average then! A remarkable number from one of the greatest ever sportspeople to have graced any pitch.

Ajit Agarkar, a former team-mate of mine, is not a name that ranks amongst the greats of the game. He was a very good cricketer who played for India over 200 times across all three formats. Sadly, he's less remembered for his Test match batting average of 16.79 or his 288 one-day international wickets. He's probably never mentioned as a batsman who scored a century at Lord's (unlike Tendulkar, Ponting, Lara and Gavaskar, unbelievably). The numbers that are forever etched against his name are 0 0 0 0 0 0 0. I'm not even sure that's a number. But it is the run of batting scores he achieved against Australia in seven consecutive innings. I feel for him. This infamous run of noughts earned him the nickname 'Bombay Duck'. He can only thank his lucky stars that this all happened before social media was a thing. I can't imagine what the internet would have thrown at him today with that run of form.

Pragyan Ojha was a generous man. So generous in fact that he allowed himself to be at the other end of another amazing number. He became Muttiah Muralitharan's 800th scalp to ensure that the little man became the only bowler in Test match history to claim 800 wickets.

Given my own personal highest score is 114, Brian Lara's 400 not out for the West Indies remains one of cricket's greatest numbers and greatest cricketing records. It is, I believe, the hardest number now in cricket for any batsman to beat and I doubt that I will see it again in my lifetime. There are hundreds of fantastic stats in cricket and many books about those stats. So, I don't need to add anything more to this body of work. Suffice to say; if ever there's a game in which numbers rule, cricket is it.

It's against this background that I came into the world of business; driven by numbers in cricket and with an already established Olympic standard in mental maths, as I mentioned in the first chapter. I remember many times during my cricket career wondering why the non-playing staff at Middlesex never seemed to be judged with the same level of scrutiny on their numbers. Given they could look at our averages and numbers every week, surely we should be able to do the same with them? Just as I was judged on the number of runs I scored and catches I took, so should a CEO of any cricket club be judged on their numbers. Revenue, gross profit, net profit and wage bill.

I can honestly say that in all the time I spent at Lord's, I could count on the fingers of no hands the numbers of times the players went through the club's numbers in any detail with the CEO. Not just the finances but other areas of growth, such as membership and merchandise. I hope that's changed now because it's one way that you could immediately build a more robust culture. Develop open and honest communication between both the playing and non-playing sides of the club around everyone's numbers. I think boards and leadership groups believe that the players don't have much to offer when it comes to having a commercial perspective. They, therefore, never ask for their advice as often as they should. In my experience, behind closed doors, there are lots of good ideas from all quarters about how to develop most cricket clubs. You just need an environment and a culture that's willing to be open enough to embrace that. It comes back to that issue of growth mindset and how far you're eager to embrace the new. I do worry that too many boards of cricket clubs today may have the opposite instinct.

My love of numbers, cricket or otherwise, has only grown over the years. As we've built our business, I've become much more adept at asking for the right numbers. I can now interpret them in the right way and use them to build a business with longevity.

One of the most impressive numbers men I've ever met is Hilton Nathanson. Hilton came over from Perth and made a fortune through his hedge fund, Marble Bar. He also set up a charitable trust to support the less privileged. He subsequently became a good mate and someone who shares the love of our great game. So much so that he asked me to coach the British Jewish Olympic cricket squad at the 2013 Maccabiah Games in Jerusalem and Tel Aviv. In some ways, not my finest moment. The *Ham & High* newspaper called to ask my thoughts on the upcoming tournament. Without thinking about the context, I said that I would repay Hilton's faith by winning a medal. If only I'd stopped there, all would have been sweet. However, my next observation about bringing home the bacon was a little misjudged to say the least. Still, you live and learn. Walking out with the British flag on our chests at the opening and closing ceremonies at Teddy Stadium in front of 36,000 people remains one of the highlights of my life.

Cricket taught me to be exact with the numbers. Now, in our company, I'm as fixated with the pennies as I was on my batting average. If I can squeeze another drop out of a deal, I will. I enjoy doing the deal of course, but I also know that every penny saved in that conversation is a penny that I can spend elsewhere in the business. It's one of the things that I've grown to understand about business. As I was told once by a mate with a great deal of money, 'No one ever shrunk their way to greatness.' He was right. I now know that the only way to move from a lifestyle business to one with real potential is to invest in the areas that you believe will generate further growth. In our business, I find most of those things very dull because they include finance systems, processes, technology and corporate governance. But the process of learning about them taught me a valuable lesson, and that is about the relationship between growth and infrastructure.

Most entrepreneurs love growth, think lots about how to achieve it and, through sheer will, the good ones make it happen. The infrastructure to support that growth isn't something that most entrepreneurs are either interested in or want to focus on. Knowing that helps you build the right resource and plan, and I've seen many a business fail because they don't understand that. My final observation about numbers is as a shareholder. Many people like to focus on revenue and profit as crucial indicators of how you assess what comes next for any business. Of course, that's a massive part of the framework through which you make your critical decisions. In my experience, many of our ex-colleagues used to forget that we are the major shareholders. Ultimately, what may be happening to us in any given year is the start-point for the conversation about what the business does. Do we need more or less cash from the company this year and why? Do we want to invest in anything outside of our core business? There could myriad of different reasons but what's right for the shareholders of any company has to be the first and most crucial start-point. We care about building our company more than anyone. Still, we are also the people who have risked everything to start it and invested our time and money into it.

If this country needs anything over the next decade, it needs more entrepreneurs. They create jobs, opportunities and wealth for people. That will only happen if you continue to make wealth creation a positive force for good in society. I'm incredibly proud of the business we've built over the last nine years. Still, I'm also proud that I've been able to create a life for myself and my family as a result of the risks I've taken. Without focusing on the numbers as closely as I have, none of that would have happened.

Chapter Twelve

Mopping Up the Tail

FOR THOSE of you steeped in cricket, you'll know that 'mopping up the tail' is a well-known phrase. It describes the process of bowling out the last vestiges of a team. In this chapter, I'm going to mop up my tail. That is to say, there are a few learnings and a few general observations that I want to make that didn't neatly fit into any of the chapters I've written. Some of them get a mention in this book, but I don't focus on them as much as I will here. So, they are the stragglers or the tail-enders if you like. Some are personal, and some are professional. My only hope is that they prove to be a bit more useful to you than most tail-enders in my experience. Here's a potpourri of opinion, observation and hopes for the game of cricket itself.

Before I move on to those, I'd just like to thank (or more likely congratulate!) you for reading this far. I'll probably never write another book again (although I have to say that I've enjoyed the challenge) and that's probably good news for the publishing world. My hope for this book was simple. I wanted to frame some of the very many experiences and learnings I've had in cricket and business to make you think and occasionally smile. I was never the world's greatest cricketer. I'm certainly not the world's most exceptional businessman. But if this book has given you the occasional insight into something that you might want to explore further, I'll be delighted. If it's managed to tell you something that you didn't know already, I'll be amazed but equally delighted. In the end, none of us has a monopoly on wisdom, and I hope some of the areas I've touched on will be worth debating if we ever have a beer at Lord's together. I'd undoubtedly enjoy that because I've become a much more informed person over the years through debate and discussion. It's one of the very many things I enjoy about meeting new people.

As I was making my way in professional cricket, little did I know that, some 20 years later, I'd be writing a book. And never one that covered leadership, the Japanese concept of *kaizen* and a model I've developed called ADAM for how companies can create momentum and focus on measurement. I certainly didn't imagine I'd be fascinated by the topic of purpose and its role in all our lives. Although I instinctively knew what poor culture looked like, I could never have imagined myself writing about it. That's true too for the role that psychological safety plays in teams and the role of numbers and mentors in business and cricket. But, touch on all of these subjects I have, and I've enjoyed thinking about all of them. Perhaps one of my hopes for the next 20 years of my journey is that it conjures up ten more topics to fill the pages of another book. We'll see.

The future of cricket is at a crossroads, and the new hundred-ball competition will now start in 2021. I do think the future of our game is in excellent hands. Tom Harrison, the ECB CEO, an excellent cricketer himself, is a great guy. He's very straight, he works hard, and he knows the game inside and out. I don't subscribe to the views of many that this new format is a gimmick that won't work. It has already worked given the extra monies that will come into the game as a result of it. It's also going to guarantee more opportunity for more players through the new 50-over competition. Again, I don't agree with the drains who say that it's going to be a devalued competition. I'd prefer to see the glass half-full view. Let's celebrate the chance that players who otherwise would be playing yet more second XI cricket will get on a slightly bigger stage. That has to be a good thing. My only hope for the new competition is that the franchises continue to be brave in their selection policies. Let's see a raft of fresh faces and a raft of young ones, too. I hope players of all shapes and sizes put themselves forward in the coming years.

County Championship cricket is at a crossroads as well, and while I can't use the pages of this book to solve its future entirely, I will say this: without someone working hard to promote it, no one new is ever going to come and watch it. I can't remember the last time I saw an interesting piece of marketing for the County Championship. The new 'Road to Lord's' finale to the 2021 season represents a very good opportunity to produce some fresh and engaging content so I hope that happens. I also worry that clubs aren't doing enough to attract new, younger members. Everyone knows this is a problem, but again, I don't see many examples of clubs trying anything new and different with any degree of consistency. Why Middlesex haven't done more to engage the massive Asian population in London, for example, is beyond me. I hope I'm wrong, but unless a coherent strategy comes alive to promote the new format of the four-day game actively, I don't see how it can survive in its current form. Urgent action is needed to give as much thought to this as all other forms of the game. Marketing is key.

On the subject of marketing, it's one of D&G's best tools currently. We do it pretty well because I think we've worked out that the key to good marketing is our ability to create exciting content and tell a story. We've got a good and authentic back story – starting from Mum and Dad's spare bedroom and in nine years raising over £20m for charity. We also encourage our teams to do everything they can to give back, and that creates excellent content too.

It's struck me over the years that marketing is key to building a successful business. It sits alongside five other things that provide me, at least, with a focus on how I look at my company. I think they're a useful guide generally. Alongside marketing, two other areas begin with m and three start with p. Nashy's three m's and p's if you like. You can put those alongside ADAM and my mentor matrix. Maybe I am a business guru after all! Of course, I'm not but here goes. The other two m's are money and mood, and we spent a fair bit of the last chapter going over money. Mood is interesting, though, as a definition of how people feel about where they work. I still like Bain's (the management consulting firm who created it) 'net promoter score' concept as the most simple guide to how you can tell how happy people are. 'Would you recommend working here to a friend or colleague?' Answer one to ten, ten being definitely. I've seen this work in so many other organisations that I should really do it in my own company and do an external one too for our clients.

There's also been much talk recently about the slightly fluffy (for some) issue of happiness in the workplace. I don't think it's fluffy at all; it is the very opposite. I see it as the single most crucial factor in business over the next decade. As artificial intelligence changes the way we work, we are all going to have to redefine what work means to us. More and more opportunities will be given to young people to choose radically different careers. As a result, employers are going to have to find ways of engaging and keeping people in their company. I sense that young people today just won't put up with the bullshit that employers used to get away with. If your environment isn't right and you are not happy in your work, you will move on. I like the challenge this presents for a business like mine, and I don't mind trying to meet it head-on.

Jacinda Ardern, the New Zealand prime minister, is leading the way in this area. Already, she has set her country on a radically different path to how they measure success. Forget gross domestic product. She's interested in gross domestic happiness and has committed significant monies to a well-being budget. There's a woman who knows how important the mood of her nation is and how it's linked to how happy and well her people feel to make progress. If her country can do it, I'm sure businesses can too. The three p's (to get back to my original point) are people, product and process. Alongside money, mood and marketing, I believe they are the six cornerstones of any business. To thrive, your business has to make progress across all of them, all of the time.

One of the areas I've touched on in the book already is instinct. As a cricketer, you have to have it just to get through a day's play. Still, you develop it quickly because of the number of different people that you meet of whom you have to make an assessment. Sport allows you to develop a considerable amount of people skills and I'm sure it's one of the reasons that I've become good at building relationships with people. It certainly helped my benefit year as I've already said. At the time, I had a good relationship with

Adam Applegarth, the then CEO of Northern Rock. My instinct told me that he was a great guy, and so it proved. Despite their business supporting Paul Collingwood's benefit year at the time, Adam still sent me a cheque for £10,000 to thank me for all that I'd done for him as a sponsor. Shortly after that, of course, Northern Rock sank as a result of the crash in 2008. I guess there are two lessons in this story. Firstly, trust your instincts about people and secondly, always cash your cheques quickly (which I did!).

In the changing room, there are no hiding places, and given how much time you spend together as cricketers, you learn how to develop relationships that go beyond the superficial. I've already talked about the role that John King, the then CEO of House of Fraser, played in our start as a business. John is perhaps the single reason why we were able to even think about growing D&G. A fantastic businessman and an even better person, John gave us a chance. We had no other credentials to show him. We hadn't worked with any other clients in doing what we were asking him to let us do. But his instinct was that I was a winner (his words not mine) who would work harder than anyone else to make sure that I didn't let him down. He wasn't wrong about my work ethic nor our ability to deliver for him.

We had an incredible few years supporting House of Fraser until they were taken over by Sports Direct. It was then that I came across Mike Ashley in what was, by some considerable margin, the most extraordinary meeting of my business life. We had two years left to run on our contract, and I needed to get some clarity on where we stood. We met Mike through one of my closest mates in business, Simon Duncan, our client at House of Fraser who had moved over to work with Mike after the sale. We wanted to show him what we did. I knew in advance that he didn't take any prisoners and so it turned out. I'd done my homework on Mike through a mate of mine, Warren Llambias, whose dad had been Mike's CEO at Newcastle.

Having been kept waiting nearly three hours, I eventually found myself sitting in front of Mike. Three minutes into telling him about our business and what we did (I'd only planned five minutes given what I'd heard of him), he stopped me and turned to Simon. Expletives rained down on all of us in a withering and brutal attack on how Simon could think about introducing us into the business when House of Fraser was performing so poorly. The level of Simon's intellect and whether he had a father all came up with a few choice Anglo-Saxon words from Mike, who then stood up to leave. At that point, Mike turned to me with a beaming smile and told me how good it was to meet me and how good our model and our purpose were. He told me that it wasn't right for House of Fraser but might be for Sports Direct and that he'd be in touch. It was almost like Jekyll had entered the room and Hyde was leaving it. I didn't see or hear from Mike Ashley again, and surprise, surprise, Simon Duncan left the business soon afterwards, along with our relationship with House of Fraser. As I walked back from the meeting that day, knowing that I would have a story to tell if nothing else, I did reflect on something. The beginning of our relationship with House of Fraser was very different to the end. Business can be a funny old thing at times.

I recently read a book on leadership. The only reason that I did was because it had 'no bullshit leadership' in its title. In fact, it was called *No Bullshit Leadership* and was by an adman called Chris Hirst. I'll come back to the book in a minute, but I love no bullshit as a thought. I liked it when I was a cricketer, and I like it in business. As a cricketer, there was no room for hiding. You either got runs, or you didn't. The team either won or it didn't. There was always a person in the changing room who would give you five reasons why they weren't performing, but no one took any notice.

Straussy is no bullshitter, and neither is Gus Fraser. Maybe that's why I get on with both of them so well. The truth is that most things are more straightforward than people pretend, and that includes leadership. The book I mentioned makes the obvious point that the bullshit that surrounds the subject of leadership inhibits any individual from fulfilling their potential. It also excludes people from believing that they too could lead. No one is a born leader, and there's no leadership type, the book argues. I suspect this is true. My business is full of people who lead, but they would not necessarily see themselves as leaders. That's a problem and almost certainly means that they don't think about what their type of leadership might mean for them and the people they influence.

One of the kindest things that people have said about me over the years is that I always take people as I find them. That's true, and I've learned over the years that it's really important to treat people in the same way, no matter who they are. I once heard a CEO refer to himself as 'the first among equals' and I think it's a brilliant way to build respect and loyalty. I also know that, without looking after the stewards at Lord's, there's no way I'd have been the first and last person ever to get into the pavilion in my suit and flip flops. Yes, of course, my coach, the CEO and the boys were vital to me at Middlesex. What mattered as much to me though were the staff making the real difference every day at Lord's. I still feel the same way today about the clients we work with and the partners we have. If you treat everyone with respect, you get a great deal more back. As Rudyard Kipling once famously wrote:

> If you can talk with crowds and keep your virtue,
> Or walk with Kings – nor lose the common touch,
> If neither foes nor loving friends can hurt you,
> If all men count with you, but none too much;
> If you can fill the unforgiving minute
> With sixty seconds' worth of distance run,
> Yours is the earth and everything that's in it.

In other words, it's not what you've got that counts; it's who you are and what you give. That's undoubtedly one of life's great lessons.

Afterword

AS A CONCLUSION to this book, I'm going to focus on what the future might hold for me, D&G and how I hope our business might evolve. We are also in the worst pandemic of our lifetime. So, I'm going to offer some brief thoughts on that too. It's an incredibly tough time for companies everywhere.

One day, I'd like to sell my business, not because I want to retire to the beach but because I'm sure there will come a time when fresh thinking and fresh legs will make a big difference to our future. We've recently appointed a new chairman, and that's given us all a big lift. Our last chairman, Mike Tobin, was brilliant as I've already discussed in an earlier chapter. He was what we needed for the first stage of our journey. I'm pleased we've got a clear purpose; to give something back. It's an easy one to work out in terms of how we grow. We'd like to help more companies give something back. We'd like to help more charities get something back. We'd also like to find other sectors that we find interesting and come up with ways of launching businesses in those sectors that also give something back. Finally, we know that the international market could be a great one for us to go after. So, hopefully, our business planning over the next few years is in good shape. As well as getting the planning right, we have to make sure that we continue to work hard and not take anything for granted. I hope our people continue to grow and find ways of using D&G to give them purpose and to help them work out what next. We certainly won't be able to keep all of our very talented people forever. Still, I hope we can persuade them to stay for as long as they enjoy it and find it stimulating.

The pandemic is going to make the process of keeping those people even harder. As I finish this book in lockdown, I've no idea how that is going to pan out. Our business is in the worst of all places currently. It revolves around retail clients predominantly, mass gatherings for our events, the generosity of people with disposable income and the existence of charities. I guess you'd call that the perfect pandemic storm. Yes, it's going to be tough for us and all of our people.

Still, I will try to do all I can to continue to communicate what I know about the future to all of our staff and to treat them with the respect that they deserve. I'm having to use quite a few of the lessons I've learned in this book in a very short space of time.

Despite the difficulties, I feel very optimistic about the future for our business and my other ventures generally. We've seen already that many companies are using the pandemic to look closely at their operations. I have friends with companies who are now doing much more business online which represents a massive opportunity for them post the pandemic. It will be more cost-effective for them to run their businesses that way, and they might find new customers too. I have noticed local businesses delivering more, and we know that some companies are thriving in this period. Zoom is the obvious example, but I was chatting to the owner of a pest control business on the phone the other day. His company is booming. More people at home means more people are hearing the ominous scratching or buzzing in the eaves. At Middlesex, we've found a fantastic way of keeping in touch with our members. I suggested to Steven Fletcher, the head of marketing at Middlesex, that we should do a series of 'Legends' Zoom calls, involving a host of ex-players sharing stories and generally having a catch-up. We did them, and they were brilliant. Again, we'd never have thought of doing that unless we were in lockdown.

In an earlier chapter, I mentioned the book I'd read which was called *A Beautiful Constraint*, which argues that creativity is at its peak when limits exist for people and business. Well, the pandemic is perhaps the ultimate example of a beautiful constraint for all of us. I, for one, am looking forward to the process of examining everything about our business and our business model in the coming weeks and months. I hope that examination will lead us to become more agile and more hungry as we emerge from this period. We certainly went into the period being as honest and as transparent as we could and I now know that all of our staff really appreciated that. We were honest with them about our prospects and straightforward enough to explain how tough things might be. My view was that it was right to do that sooner rather than later and I'm glad we did. It helped give everyone direction and clear guidance on their future.

During this period in our business, new leaders have emerged too. Neil Maclaurin, the chairman of our recently launched hospitality business and ex-MD of Keith Prowse, has been a revelation. He helped with the overall scenario planning on our lockdown strategy, gave us invaluable strategic advice about our future direction and was a fantastic sounding board generally. A real reminder that mentors do matter.

My heart goes out to the vast number of people around the world who have suffered loss, illness and real hardship during this period. It's been unimaginably tough for some people. Mum and Dad are staring down the barrel of a few more months in lockdown possibly, so that weighs heavily on my mind. As we all consider our response to what we've witnessed, I know for my part that I will keep giving back. I'll also keep looking for ways to support the most vulnerable in our society through the work we do and the people we support. For many people, the lockdown has been a period to reflect and take stock of their lives, and I'm no different.

Fundamentally, I've realised that I am all of the things that I talk about in this book. I am ambitious, I love a challenge, I like to be busy, and I love people. It has, though, also allowed me to realise the real value of the time that you spend with your family. The spontaneous moments are the ones you sometimes get most from. I've loved hearing birdsong again, and I've loved not seeing the skies full of planes. I've enjoyed catching up with friends, especially ones I haven't seen for a while, all thanks to the wonders of technology. I've also enjoyed a bit of slow living for a change. I couldn't do it forever though, not least because Jules would kill me if I were in the house all the time. Finally, I've enjoyed the opportunity to get together with Lacey online and finish this book. In all honesty, it's one of the things that has kept me going and, in that regard, I'm fortunate. The book has given me real purpose (there's that theme again) and that has made all the difference. It is another excellent example of why having a purpose matters.

I think, for all of us, the pandemic has been an opportunity to learn new things and think about what we've seen globally. I have a few real hopes when we come out of the other side. My sense in this period is that the good people have got better and the bad ones worse. By that I mean that we've seen people with essential goodness in them, just get better and better. There are so many examples of this but one stands out. Six months ago, we pitched some hospitality ideas to the Brimelow family who run a business in Manchester called Duo. Nothing came of that pitch but during lockdown, I received a call from Anthony Brimelow. What he said astounded me. He was sending us a cheque for £25,000 because he imagined that our business may be struggling in terms of cashflow and he was keen to do business with us in the future. So much so that he wanted to put monies on account with us for future events. It was an extraordinarily kind and thoughtful gesture from a client whom I hope we can work with for many years to come.

The big issue is that the wrong 'uns in our society have got worse during the pandemic. The cyclists who think they own the towpath. The joggers who believe they can empty the contents of their noses while running. The people who think it's an opportunity to steal from empty shops and the rich celebrities and billionaires who think it's okay to use taxpayers' money to prop their businesses up. None of it is right, and the pandemic has brought the worst out in some people. It's been disheartening to witness how some people have responded to the biggest crisis in my lifetime.

Not the case, though, for our NHS and its workers. They have all been incredible, and there isn't anyone in this country who doesn't owe them an enormous debt of gratitude. I hope and pray that the NHS is never taken for granted again. It needs real funding, of course, but it also needs to take this opportunity to set out a strategy for its future and a roadmap to futureproof its existence. If we've learned anything from this pandemic, it's that we were not as ready as we should have been for the initial rush of cases. Let's hope that we never fall into this trap again. I think, given Boris Johnson's near-death experience, that he will prioritise the NHS more than anything else during his time as PM. I only hope that we remember this period and what the NHS has done for us, for many decades and not just years to come.

As well as NHS workers, we've seen some extraordinary levels of kindness and amazing human stories. Captain Tom is chief among them of course, but the mantra surely for this pandemic is that kindness wins. I think we've all been reminded that this is one of the great truisms of life and I hope we all carry on behaving that way every day from now on. I'm proud that, during this period, we've also managed to give something back. We've raised just over £28,000 for the NHS and for the Ruth Strauss Foundation through what turned out to be one of the most enjoyable nights in lockdown. Great mates like Rory Bremner gave their time for free to provide a much-needed online evening of laughs and light-hearted banter.

From my perspective, this period has reminded me of a few invaluable lessons in business. Honesty has paid dividends during the lockdown period. While my team know that I don't have all of the answers, I've needed to be as straight with them as I can be. They have mouths to feed and bills to pay, and they need as much information as possible to make their medium-term plans. I've also been reminded that the best relationships come to the fore in the bad times. I've been truly humbled by the way that our clients have responded to our current constraints. I'm not going to name you because that would be unfair to the people who, for very good reason, haven't been able to help. However, to those who have helped us and you know who you are, thank you so much. I've always known that we've got great people and brilliant clients and this lockdown period has highlighted that and more.

For me now, my life moving forward will be about looking after my family, rebuilding the business I love and continuing my other entrepreneurial ventures. Over the coming years, I'd like those ventures to define me more than D&G does currently. I now have business interests in property, retail and a communications agency. This diversification of my business interests will allow me to take advantage of the many opportunities that I see emerging over the next few years. It will be a chance for me to take greater managed risks and to invest with people who have the same values as me. I love investing in businesses with people who share my passion for risk and reward. I call that 'hurt money' and in my experience, the best investment partnerships are ones in which all parties have something important to lose.

I've got that with Ajay Gokani, a fellow investor and entrepreneur, who has taught me more about the art of the entrepreneurial deal than almost anyone else. So, I'd like to do more of that with more people because I think it's what's going to get me up in the mornings for the next 30 years. As I've said already, anyone who fancies a chat can call anytime. My final hope is that, whatever happens, I keep learning and I keep failing. That may sound strange, but I think failing forward is one of the keys to being successful. In the end, you are defined in business by your ratio of successes to failures. I'm planning on staying on the right side of that line!

So far, I've achieved more than I could ever have thought possible. A professional cricket career in which I made lifelong friends, all of whom have helped me write this book in so many different ways. A business that we've built from scratch that now gets my juices flowing every day and most recently, having completed building something else. A new house, in my beloved Sunbury and something that will be a legacy for our children. I'm proud to have done all of this while remembering my roots. Our FNBC (Friday Night Boys' Club) at The White Horse pub with the lads I've known for years in Sunbury is alive and well. The likes of The Gimp, Senny, Chelsea Dan and Danger Granger all keep me honest although not necessarily sober! Don't ask me why these lunatics have the nicknames they do; I've known them for so long that I've forgotten. There's so much more to achieve, and I'm looking forward to the next chapter of it all and to, hopefully, giving back even more over the next ten years.

I hope you've enjoyed reading this book half as much as I've enjoyed writing it. I also hope that it's given you food for thought along the way. No book like this would be complete though without one final word of advice. For that, I'm going to leave you with the words of the late, great Don McCarthy, the brilliant House of Fraser chairman. It's possibly the only advice you should heed in this book:

'Nashy, son, remember these three things and you'll be fine,' he once told me. 'Get amazing people around you, always go with your gut feel and when you go to see your bank manager, always whack your best suit on.'

South Africa Under-15s v England Under-15s

England Under-15s in South Africa 1992/93 (3rd ODI)
Centurion Park, Verwoerdburg on 20th March 1993 (55-over match)
England Under-15s won by losing fewer wickets

South Africa Under-15s innings

V Masingata	run out	37
MS Taliep	c Nash b Batty	41
B Lowen	run out	53
R Munnik	c Webster b Feather	21
H van Vuuren	c Flintoff b Feather	3
S Hofmeyr	c Nash b Webster	22
*+BW van Beuge	c and b Batty	6
B Zibane	run out	3
J Garland	c Feather b Webster	1
NF Alberts	run out	3
I Mitchell	not out	0
Extras	(1 b, 7 lb, 1 nb, 14 w)	23
Total	(all out, 55 overs)	213

Fall of wickets: 1-79, 2-89, 3-142, 4-152, 5-192 (55 ov), 6-204, 7-208, 8-209, 9-213, 10-213 (55 ov)

England	O	M	R	W
Webster	11	0	33	2
Tudor	11	1	41	0
Kirkland	11	3	24	0
Sales	4	0	26	0
Batty	11	0	46	2
Feather	6	0	29	2
Flintoff	1	0	3	0

England Under-15s innings

*M Snell	b Alberts	4
S Widdup	run out	3
+DC Nash	not out	60
DJG Sales	c van Beuge b Munnik	0
GJ Batty	c van Beuge b van Vuuren	0
A Flintoff	not out	132
JN Webster	did not bat	
AJ Tudor	did not bat	
D Kirkland	did not bat	
ZR Feather	did not bat	
BV Taylor	did not bat	
Extras	(1 b, 5 lb, 8 w)	14
Total	(4 wickets, innings closed, 55 overs)	213

Fall of wickets: 1-7, 2-9, 3-9, 4-12

South Africa	O	M	R	W
Alberts	11	3	41	1
Munnik	11	4	36	1
van Vuuren	11	0	60	1
Taliep	11	3	18	0
Garland	11	0	52	0

Somerset v Middlesex

AXA Equity and Law League 1995
County Ground, Taunton on 17th September 1995 (40-over match)
Somerset won the toss and decided to bat
Middlesex won by 7 wickets (Run rate)
Umpires: MJ Kitchen, PB Wight

Somerset innings		
MN Lathwell	lbw b DJ Nash	1
ME Trescothick	c Brown b Follett	5
PCL Holloway	b Follett	3
RJ Harden	c DC Nash b DJ Nash	4
KA Parsons	c DC Nash b Fraser	25
GD Rose	c Weekes b Rashid	28
Mushtaq Ahmed	st DC Nash b Rashid	5
*AN Hayhurst	c Follett b Weekes	8
+RJ Turner	c Ramprakash b Fraser	19
JID Kerr	c Gatting b Fraser	6
HRJ Trump	not out	6
Extras	(1 b, 5 lb, 4 nb, 12 w)	22
Total	(all out, 36.4 overs)	132

Fall of wickets: 1-1, 2-14, 3-19, 4-20, 5-72, 6-86, 7-89, 8-114, 9-116, 10-132 (36.4 ov)

Middlesex	O	M	R	W
Follett	7	1	27	2
DJ Nash	6	0	13	2
Weekes	8	1	21	1
Rashid	8	1	38	2
Fraser	7.4	0	27	3

Middlesex innings		
PN Weekes	c Parsons b Kerr	23
KR Brown	c Turner b Rose	12
JD Carr	c Trump b Rose	3
JC Pooley	not out	40
MR Ramprakash	not out	23
*MW Gatting	did not bat	
DJ Nash	did not bat	
+DC Nash	did not bat	
UBA Rashid	did not bat	
ARC Fraser	did not bat	
D Follett	did not bat	
Extras	(6 lb, 7 w)	13
Total	(3 wickets, 21 overs)	114

Fall of wickets: 1-26, 2-34, 3-65

Somerset	O	M	R	W
Rose	7	1	28	2
Mushtaq Ahmed	6	0	20	0
Trump	4	0	16	0
Kerr	4	0	44	1

Pakistan Under-19s v England Under-19s

England Under-19s in Pakistan 1996/97 (2nd Test)
Sheikhupura Stadium, Sheikhupura on 19th, 20th, 21st, 22nd December 1996 (4-day match)
England Under-19s won the toss and decided to bat
Match drawn
Umpires: Azhar Hasan, Rab Nawaz

England Under-19s first innings

SD Peters	c Farhan Adil b Jannisar Khan	74
JA Graham	b Abdur Razzaq	2
DJG Sales	lbw b Abdur Razzaq	6
*A Flintoff	c Humayun Farhat b Abdur Razzaq	33
+DC Nash	not out	108
BC Hollioake	b Abdur Razzaq	37
CMW Read	lbw b Hasan Raza	45
GJ Batty	c Humayun Farhat b Abdur Razzaq	1
AJ Tudor	b Abdur Razzaq	10
JC Powell	c Humayun Farhat b Abdur Razzaq	0
DA Cosker	lbw b Imran Tahir	5
Extras	(14 b, 9 lb, 12 nb, 5 w)	40
Total	(all out, 130.3 overs)	361

Fall of wickets: 1-18, 2-30, 3-108, 4-153, 5-224, 6-317, 7-326, 8-347, 9-347, 10-361 (130.3 ov)

Pakistan	O	M	R	W
Abdur Razzaq	38	9	118	7
Jannisar Khan	17	2	32	1
Imran Tahir	33.3	8	82	1
Fahad Khan	33	6	85	0
Shadab Kabir	5	0	12	0
Hasan Raza	4	1	9	1

Pakistan Under-19s first innings

Saeed Anwar	c Read b Tudor	5
Shahid Qambrani	c Read b Hollioake	20
Farhan Adil	c Flintoff b Tudor	12
Mohammad Saleem	run out	1
Hasan Raza	c Cosker b Tudor	0
*Shadab Kabir	c Hollioake b Powell	30
Jannisar Khan	c Flintoff b Hollioake	0
+Humayun Farhat	c Read b Hollioake	32
Abdur Razzaq	c Read b Tudor	85
Fahad Khan	not out	18
Imran Tahir	b Tudor	0
Extras	(9 b, 6 lb, 4 w)	19
Total	(all out, 92.5 overs)	222

Fall of wickets: 1-16, 2-42, 3-46, 4-47, 5-49, 6-51, 7-99, 8-137, 9-218, 10-222 (92.5 ov)

England	O	M	R	W
Tudor	23.5	6	52	5
Hollioake	27	9	63	3
Cosker	20	5	50	0
Batty	4	1	10	0
Powell	18	7	32	1

Pakistan Under-19s v England Under-19s

England Under-19s in Pakistan 1996/97 (3rd ODI)
National Stadium, Karachi on 8th January 1997 (50-over match)
Pakistan Under-19s won by 2 wickets
Umpires: Saleem Badar, Shakeel Khan

England Under-19s innings

SD Peters	b Fazl-e-Akbar	25
JA Graham	c Mohammad Farrukh b Fazl-e-Akbar	51
DJG Sales	b Fazl-e-Akbar	0
A Flintoff	c Mohammad Saleem b Shoaib Malik	18
BC Hollioake	c Mohammad Shakeel b Saeed Anwar	1
+DC Nash	b Abdur Razzaq	76
GJ Batty	run out	16
ZC Morris	not out	15
AJ Tudor	not out	0
JC Powell	did not bat	
SRG Francis	did not bat	
Extras	(1 b, 8 lb, 1 nb, 19 w)	29
Total	(7 wickets, innings closed, 50 overs)	231

Fall of wickets: 1-50, 2-54, 3-93, 4-96, 5-138, 6-175, 7-223

Pakistan	O	M	R	W
Abdur Razzaq	10	1	48	1
Waqas Ahmed	10	1	52	0
Fazl-e-Akbar	10	2	29	3
Shoaib Malik	10	0	51	1
Saeed Anwar	10	0	42	1

Pakistan Under-19s innings

Saeed Anwar	c Nash b Tudor	0
Mohammad Farrukh	lbw b Tudor	21
Waqas Ahmed	b Hollioake	14
Hasan Raza	c Flintoff b Hollioake	16
Mohammad Saleem	b Francis	9
*Ahmer Saeed	run out	63
Farhan Adil	run out	66
Abdur Razzaq	not out	16
+Mohammad Shakeel	c Batty b Tudor	7
Shoaib Malik	not out	2
Fazl-e-Akbar	did not bat	
Extras	(3 b, 13 lb, 1 nb, 4 w)	21
Total	(8 wickets, 49.5 overs)	235

Fall of wickets: 1-0, 2-21, 3-50, 4-59, 5-80, 6-208, 7-214, 8-223

England	O	M	R	W
Tudor	10	1	43	3
Hollioake	9.5	1	52	2
Francis	8	0	22	1
Batty	8	0	28	0
Powell	7	0	39	0
Morris	7	0	35	0

Middlesex v Somerset

Britannic Assurance County Championship 1998
Lord's Cricket Ground, St John's Wood on 13th, 14th, 15th, 16th May 1998 (4-day match)
Middlesex won the toss and decided to bat
Middlesex won by 211 runs
Umpires: DJ Constant, JW Lloyds

Middlesex second innings

RA Kettleborough	c Turner b Caddick	19
JL Langer	not out	233
MW Gatting	b Caddick	20
OA Shah	lbw b Caddick	0
DC Nash	c Burns b Trescothick	114
*+KR Brown	not out	45
ARC Fraser	did not bat	
JP Hewitt	did not bat	
RL Johnson	did not bat	
PCR Tufnell	did not bat	
PN Weekes	did not bat	
Extras	(1 b, 10 lb, 8 nb)	19
Total	(4 wickets, declared, 130.5 overs)	450

Fall of wickets: 1-42 (Kettleborough), 2-101 (Gatting), 3-109 (Shah), 4-331 (Nash)

Somerset bowling	O	M	R	W
Caddick	33	6	118	3
Shine	20	2	86	0
Rose	25.5	5	94	0
Mushtaq Ahmed	30	8	76	0
Trescothick	16	2	36	1
Parsons	6	0	29	0

Somerset second innings

*PD Bowler	c Gatting b Fraser	21
M Burns	c Langer b Hewitt	8
KA Parsons	c Shah b Johnson	4
RJ Harden	lbw b Fraser	2
MN Lathwell	c Nash b Hewitt	88
+RJ Turner	c Nash b Fraser	1
KJ Shine	c Kettleborough b Fraser	2
ME Trescothick	c Hewitt b Johnson	3
GD Rose	c Kettleborough b Tufnell	16
Mushtaq Ahmed	c Weekes b Tufnell	12
AR Caddick	not out	15
Extras	(4 b, 10 lb, 4 nb)	18
Total	(all out, 62 overs)	190

Fall of wickets: 1-12 (Burns), 2-31 (Parsons), 3-38 (Harden), 4-39 (Bowler), 5-47 (Turner), 6-49 (Shine), 7-56 (Trescothick), 8-97 (Rose), 9-133 (Mushtaq Ahmed), 10-190 (Lathwell, 62 ov)

Middlesex	O	M	R	W
Fraser	17	3	39	4
Hewitt	9	0	41	2
Johnson	17	4	48	2
Tufnell	13	2	34	2
Weekes	6	2	14	0

Sri Lanka A v England A

England A in Kenya and Sri Lanka 1997/98
Uyanwatte Stadium, Matara on 6th, 7th, 8th, 9th February 1998 (4-day match)
Sri Lanka A won the toss and decided to bat
England A won by 1 wicket
Umpires: RMS Sirisoma, TH Wijewardene

Sri Lanka A first innings

*RP Arnold	c Nash b Hutchison	15
DA Gunawardene	c Knight b Giles	51
MN Nawaz	c and b Giles	5
DPMD Jayawardene	c Knight b Cosker	6
BCMS Mendis	c and b Cosker	58
SI de Saram	c Maddy b Cosker	5
+PB Dassanayake	c Knight b Giles	2
JWHD Boteju	c Ealham b Hollioake	10
MRCN Bandaratilleke	not out	10
PDRL Perera	c Nash b Giles	4
MA Junaid	b Hutchison	1
Extras	(1 lb, 2 nb, 1 w)	4
Total	(all out, 72.3 overs)	171

Fall of wickets: 1-43, 2-70, 3-81, 4-85, 5-97, 6-114, 7-155, 8-157, 9-162, 10-171 (72.3 ov)

England A	O	M	R	W
Hutchison	7.3	3	25	2
Hollioake	6	1	29	1
Brown	7	2	18	0
Giles	26	7	52	4
Cosker	26	11	46	3

England A first innings

SP James	b Bandaratilleke	34
*NV Knight	lbw b Perera	0
DL Maddy	lbw b Junaid	27
MA Ealham	lbw b Junaid	6
DJG Sales	lbw b Bandaratilleke	3
BC Hollioake	c Mendis b Junaid	103
+DC Nash	lbw b Bandaratilleke	10
DR Brown	b Bandaratilleke	0
AF Giles	lbw b Boteju	39
DA Cosker	c and b Jayawardene	13
PM Hutchison	not out	11
Extras	(2 b, 10 lb, 2 w)	14
Total	(all out, 104 overs)	260

Fall of wickets: 1-1, 2-64, 3-64, 4-69, 5-93, 6-122, 7-122, 8-219, 9-229, 10-260 (104 ov)

Sri Lanka A	O	M	R	W
Perera	11	1	54	1
Boteju	12	3	19	1
Bandaratilleke	33	11	57	4
Junaid	21	3	61	3
Arnold	13	3	22	0
Jayawardene	14	2	35	1

Middlesex v Australians

Australia in British Isles 2001
Lord's Cricket Ground, St John's Wood on 5th June 2001 (50-over match)
Middlesex won the toss and decided to field
Middlesex won by 6 wickets
Umpires: B Leadbeater, AGT Whitehead

Australians innings		
ML Hayden	c Weekes b Hewitt	3
ME Waugh	c Hutton b Hewitt	14
RT Ponting	c Nash b Weekes	57
*SR Waugh	c Weekes b Keegan	4
DR Martyn	c Nash b Cook	19
A Symonds	lbw b Cook	4
IJ Harvey	b Cook	84
+WA Seccombe	c and b Weekes	9
SK Warne	c Nash b Weekes	7
JN Gillespie	not out	19
NW Bracken	b Hunt	1
Extras	(4 lb, 4 nb, 3 w)	11
Total	(all out, 44.2 overs)	232

Fall of wickets: 1-17 (Hayden), 2-36 (ME Waugh), 3-43 (SR Waugh), 4-78 (Martyn), 5-106 (Ponting), 6-108 (Symonds), 7-141 (Seccombe), 8-154 (Warne), 9-229 (Harvey), 10-232 (Bracken)

Middlesex	O	M	R	W
Hewitt	9	2	43	2
Keegan	10	2	57	1
Hunt	4.2	0	32	1
Cook	8	0	39	3
Weekes	10	0	36	3
Hutton	3	0	21	0

Middlesex innings		
AJ Strauss	c Harvey b Bracken	15
BL Hutton	run out	73
OA Shah	st Seccombe b Warne	50
RMS Weston	not out	36
SJ Cook	c Martyn b Harvey	20
MA Roseberry	not out	11
*PN Weekes	did not bat	
+DC Nash	did not bat	
CB Keegan	did not bat	
JP Hewitt	did not bat	
TA Hunt	did not bat	
Extras	(3 b, 5 lb, 5 nb, 15 w)	28
Total	(4 wickets, 47.1 overs)	233

Fall of wickets: 1-33 (Strauss), 2-146 (Shah), 3-170 (Hutton), 4-204 (Cook)

Australians	O	M	R	W
Gillespie	9	0	38	0
Bracken	8	0	47	1
Warne	10	1	39	1
Harvey	10	1	36	1
Symonds	8.1	0	54	0
Martyn	2	0	11	0

Middlesex v Kent

Frizzell County Championship 2003 (Division 1)
Lord's Cricket Ground, St John's Wood on 13th, 14th, 15th, 16th August 2003 (4-day match)
Middlesex won the toss and decided to bat
Kent won by 8 wickets
Umpires: R Palmer, AGT Whitehead

Middlesex first innings	Runs	
*AJ Strauss	c Jones b Khan	12
SG Koenig	c Ealham b Muralitharan	57
OA Shah	b Khan	0
BL Hutton	c Jones b Saggers	17
EC Joyce	b Muralitharan	43
PN Weekes	lbw b Muralitharan	11
+DC Nash	run out	113
JWM Dalrymple	c Walker b Muralitharan	5
SJ Cook	lbw b Saggers	65
CB Keegan	not out	36
JH Dawes	b Muralitharan	18
Extras	(1 b, 8 lb, 18 nb, 3 w)	30
Total	(all out, 115 overs)	407

Fall of wickets:
1-31 (Strauss), 2-35 (Shah), 3-58 (Hutton), 4-119 (Koenig), 5-149 (Weekes), 6-160 (Joyce), 7-190 (Dalrymple), 8-315 (Cook), 9-381 (Nash), 10-407 (Dawes, 115 ov)

Kent bowling	O	M	R	W
Saggers	26	3	95	2
Khan	17	1	100	2
Sheriyar	15	6	40	0
Ealham	15	3	42	0
Muralitharan	38	4	103	5
Symonds	4	1	18	0

THANK YOU
MKK